GETTING OUT
of
YOUR OWN
WAY

Unlocking Your True
Performance Potential

Nancy Shainberg

GETTING OUT OF YOUR OWN WAY
Unlocking Your True Performance Potential

by Nancy Shainberg

Published by: Luminous Press
2565 Broadway, #185
New York, NY 10025
Phone: 212-316-6648
E-mail: LuminousPress@ultinet.net

Library of Congress Control Number: 2001 126195

ISBN: 0-9708004-0-1

Printed in the United States of America

10 9 8 7 6 5 4 3 2 1

DEDICATION

Inside each of us there is something amazing. Some call this "thing" intuition; some *self* or *felt sense*, still others, *soul*. No matter what we name it, it remains the force within us that knows what is best for us, the keeper of our truth, gauge for what we really want. Sometimes this intuitive sense may feel vague, clouded or absent. Some of us may be acquainted with this personal place of knowing, others not. Regardless of our current relationship with this "thing," it is and always has been there inside us, waiting for our attention. This powerful source is always on our team; when we can tap into and follow its sense of "rightness," it will always lead us to wellness. This book is dedicated to the magical place of *knowing* that lives within us all.

~ *Nancy Shainberg*

ACKNOWLEDGMENTS

So many people have contributed to my writing this book—friends, colleagues, clients—each teaching me something priceless. I wish I could mention each by name but the list would be too long. Two people, however, stand out in my mind and heart as being integral not only to the making of this book, but also to my becoming the person who could write it. First, Rogelio Sosnik, who successfully showed me how to live a life of possibility. And Jimmy Toon, who taught me not only how to ride, but how to *be* a rider. It would be an injustice to attempt to box my appreciation in words and so, I offer a simple thank you, knowing that such feelings cannot be translated into language.

There are several other people to whom I am deeply grateful as well—those who have touched me personally and whose presence in my life has helped make this work possible:

Lynn Preston, who has taught and continues to teach me a new way of seeing. Eileen Kelly, a most wonderful friend in every way. Fred Colier, whose aliveness and passion for learning inspires me to fulfill my own greatest potential. Jan Bronson, who, with openness and kindness, consistently offers me the space to discover my own truth. And my mother, Diane Shainberg, who is a role model for involvement and endless spirit.

It is with all of my heart that I say thank you to these special people. In their unique ways, each contributes something remarkable to my life.

~ *Nancy Shainberg*

TABLE OF CONTENTS

ABOUT THE AUTHOR

Nancy Shainberg is a psychotherapist in private practice as well as the Director of Psychological Services for the Miller Health Care Institute for Performing Artists of St. Luke's Roosevelt Hospital. In addition, she competes year-round as an equestrian athlete, campaigning her three horses on the national horse show circuit. Nancy lives in Manhattan with her husband, Fred Colier and her cat, Marbella.

PREFACE

This book is a guide to opening your true performance potential. It offers a new path to awakening the very best that you have to offer. Performing at your potential does not result, as often believed, from adding new techniques or programs to a vast collection of already acquired strategies. Accessing your very best is about developing a core self that is sound and strong. When you achieve this, you will succeed.

I have been in the performance business for many years and have met with every possible type of performer. Nonetheless, I have yet to meet a highly experienced artist whose problem with succeeding originated from an external or training related issue. There arrives a stage in our performing career when we know what we are supposed to do. This is why we practice long hours, day in and day out, to become the master in our fields. Yet often, we still can't be successful, or more appropriately, won't allow ourselves to be. Adding more knowledge or techniques to practice does not make a difference. Determination, diligence, industry seem to have little effect, with the exception of growing frustration. What we need is a different approach—one that addresses the internal situation in addition to the external. These days, there are teams of experts catering to every performer; each expert with his or her own technique, method, and quick-fix system designed to make us win. The majority of these "experts," however, takes an outside-in approach, applying an external solution to what is often an internal problem. To apply something from the outside is certainly easier than to try and heal an unsound core. Unfortunately, these outside-in approaches rarely work, as they do not encourage the core's nature to change. The results are short-lived; they help for a while and then fail again when our unsound core catches up with the artful solution of the moment. After studying all the self-help books, we are armed with an arsenal of techniques while we maintain the same basic beliefs and fundamental vision of ourselves. Things may change in theory but won't change in reality unless the deepest level is explored. True brilliance within our craft can only shine when our core-self is ready.

This outside-in approach carries another hidden downside. Slapping an expert's external methods and slogans onto an internal problem teaches us not to trust ourselves—the very worst thing a performer can learn. We are, through this process, learning that we must be told what to do in order to bring out our true best—that someone else knows what is right for us. No one else knows what is best for us. Only we do. We all have an internal knowing place that too often we deny or silence because we are taught that someone else knows more or better. In fact, our intuition about our selves is our greatest source of excellence. This book is a "how-to" for locating and trusting that place of intuition within us. Until we can trust this place of knowing, we will always be operating with less than our true power.

There are parts of each of us that do not act in our own best interest, sabotaging and blocking our best efforts to succeed. Given this, it may feel safer and more prudent to trust an expert's ideas rather than our own. But as long as there is something within us not acting in our best interest we remain in trouble—our potential is blocked. No external system can overrule the negativity that lives within us. Bringing your highest potential to life requires that you become someone who believes that you are the expert in your own life and, as such, can trust what your intuition tells you. You have the answers. The challenge is in finding and trusting what is already within you.

My goal here is to help you access your own true performance potential, to facilitate your bringing out the very best in you. Unlike other experts, I am not here to provide you with a false performance-self behind which to disappear. In order to bring your very best to life, you must *be* the performer who trusts her own knowing. The process is about *being* rather than doing. But being this kind of performer is by no means a passive event. It does involve a certain kind of doing. I call this kind of doing, becoming. Becoming a performer who trusts her own knowing requires action, but it is an internal action rather than external.

My understanding of performance is a result of the life I have lived. To begin with, I have spent the last 25 years training as an equestrian athlete. For the last 15 of those years, I have ridden competitively on the national horse show "A" circuit. It was not until my late twenties, however, that I really started to win at the top level. Up until that point I was talented but couldn't turn that talent into real success. I had the skills but not the internal power or maturity to be the winner. My approach to training had been purely external. I assumed that the reason I couldn't win was because of what I was doing and not who I was. No matter how much I changed what I was doing, the results never changed. It wasn't until I shifted the focus of my training to the internal, to how I was relating to myself as a performer and my craft as a whole, that I was able to bridge the gap that was at the core of my unfulfilled potential.

In addition to my personal experience as a high level performer, professionally, I am a psychotherapist specializing in the treatment of performing artists. I have years of experience applying my personal approach to work with clients, all of whom come from radically different disciplines; music, opera, dance, athletics, writing, anything that demands the highest and most specialized level of artistic expertise. In working with these varied performers, I am continually surprised by the similarity in the issues they face. Whether you are a 40 year-old jazz musician or a 19 year-old ballerina, the walls you come up against in fulfilling your potential are the same. The walls we face as high-level performers cannot be avoided; they are an integral part of the path that is excellence. Indeed, our capacity to confront such walls is the very essence of greatness. This book addresses not only how I overcame my own personal blocks to success, but also how I am able to help my clients with the obstacles that they face. Regardless of the discipline, the path to success requires the very same ability. Every successful performer must learn to access, trust, and live her true potential. This is a skill unto itself and as such, requires its own development. This book teaches you how to accomplish just that.

~ *Nancy Shainberg*

WILLINGNESS

*Willingness is the breath of opportunity;
with it, all things are possible,
without it we are lost.*

$\sim$

Congratulations. You have taken the first step toward fulfilling your true performance potential. Given that you have opened this particular book, I am going to assume that there is some area of your performance potential that is not being fully expressed, something about the way you are currently living, training, feeling and/or thinking that needs changing. Most people respond positively when you talk to them about change. They stare at you intently, nod enthusiastically and affirm their desire to begin the process. But if you watch closely, you will see them develop a glazed expression in their eyes when you reach the part about how *they* need to change so their lives will change. This is the piece of the puzzle I call willingness. At this point, most people turn "change" into an intellectual exercise. They stop considering their role in their own transformation and become interested in "change" as an idea or concept.

People desire change; they want to live different kinds of lives. The catch is: they want it to happen *to* them—to wake up one morning feeling different with a new life. What they don't want to do is struggle and do the work that changing involves.

Why don't people want to do the work? In short, because it's hard. Changing takes great effort. It means trying something new, entering the unknown, being uncomfortable, stretching, leaving safe and familiar ground. Regardless of how unsatisfying your life may be, nonetheless, you've survived thus far. Change means saying good-bye to the you who is going to change, the *you* you know. Change means throwing out your old system without any guarantee that a new system will be any better. These are hard things to do.

And yet, if you are willing right now, this second, to commit to making the effort, to face the unknown, to make real changes in the way you think, behave, operate, relate, and in short, are, you will change your life. *You*, however, must change it, *it* will not change *for* you. There will be no morning you miraculously wake up to find a different life or a different you. Your life is not something that shows up like the morning paper; it is up to you to create the life you wake up to. If you are willing to face the struggle and do the necessary work to shed your old skin, you *will* reach your potential. If you choose to change, you *will* change, and so will your life. The whole game is about willingness; once you are truly willing, the rest will come.

GETTING OFF
THE FENCE

To choose is to live.
Have you the courage to choose your own life?

*T*he first step to change is choosing to get off the fence.
Most of the people who show up in my office, within 15
minutes, are talking about needing to "get off the fence"
in their lives. Everyone seems to be talking about "the fence"
these days. And yet, with the explosion of such "pop"
terminology, the words themselves have become a symptom of
the terminal ambivalence they seek to eradicate; their usage,
a substitute for the very change they attempt to inspire.
Using our "pop" language, it is far too easy for us to verbally
commit to change in our lives while in actuality changing
nothing. You may look and sound like you're changing but are
the words connected to anything on the inside?

ALL OF YOU

If you are one of those living your life on the fence, chances are you don't need to be informed of it. Indeed, it may feel as if you are living a paralyzed existence. What you may not know however, is the link between your success (or lack thereof) and your seat on that fence. Quite simply, playing from the fence makes reaching your potential impossible. True success (that which arises from your potential) is reserved for those who are *in* the game. True success is about *making* choices, instead of only weighing them. Getting off the fence is about getting *into* your life, committing every ounce of yourself to your passion. Mind you, this doesn't necessarily mean that you have to give up everything else in your life. It does mean that you must stop making excuses for why you can't or shouldn't give it your all. When you are there *doing it*, every ounce of you must be there *doing it*. No part of you can be missing, distracted by thoughts of where you are not, where you will be or where you already have been.

DECISIONS

So why are you still on the fence if you already know all this? Sitting on the fence is a way of staying nowhere for fear of being somewhere. The Latin root of the verb decide is "to lose." And indeed, every decision brings with it an element of loss. To decide to do and be something is simultaneously a decision *not* to do and be something else. When you allow yourself to be involved, you make the decision to *put* yourself somewhere; you decide to be *here* and not *there*. Your outline immediately changes from pencil to ink. Once you commit to being this, you can't be that. True involvement demands that you be willing to make this decision, to sacrifice what *could be* for what *is*.

Does taking on an identity and committing to something make you feel trapped or limited?

A musician explains:

> *The instant I agree to being here, to being **in this**, suddenly, I am convinced that **there** and **that** are all I ever wanted. Miraculously, **there** and **that** appear to offer a perfect and ambivalence-free life. What if I wanted to be who and where I actually am? What would that mean? What would that imply for my life? Who would that make me? Isn't it curious that my conviction for **there** develops just after I have signed the lease on **here**!*

The sad irony is that you are already trapped by precisely the hypothetical freedom that is supposed to protect you.

There you sit on the fence staring out at all the beautiful meadows you *could* be playing in. Unfortunately, you see only the fences themselves and *not* what they contain. You are correct in one sense: by choosing a meadow and deciding to *put* yourself somewhere, you are indeed agreeing to give up what's in all those other meadows. You will not get to play in *those* flowers. What you are forgetting, however, is that you *will* have all that is in *your* meadow, a quantity you can only know once you're there *in* it. By committing to nothing, you are attempting to *avoid* missing out on anything, to save yourself from ever being deprived. This is a backdoor approach to life, a life based on not *not* getting as opposed to *getting*. It's not about freedom or possibility, but about *not* being limited. The sad irony is that you are already limited by precisely the hypothetical freedom that is supposed to protect you. By attempting to hold onto the *possibility* of everything, you end up with only unfulfilled possibilities, otherwise known as *nothing*. Unwilling to close *any* of the gates, you effectively lock yourself out of a satisfying life. Don't fool yourself. The decision not to decide *is* a decision, and it's a decision to have nothing. Your system is a breeding ground for frustration. Never can you reap the rewards of involvement or commitment; never will you get to have *all* of something, just little bits and pieces of nothing. Such a system does not create a satisfying life, to say nothing of greatness.

The system rewards the brave. It is only with your feet on the meadow's grass that you can recognize *your* meadow's unlimited expanse; only from *within* it do the fences vanish and your meadow becomes infinite. Before anything can happen however, you must decide to give yourself to your passion, and to your identity as defined by that passion. Whatever you are, athlete, performer, artist, parent, friend, *be it*. Reaching your potential means agreeing to sacrifice what you *could* have for what you *can* have. As long as you are still thinking about what you're missing, what you're not doing, you're not ready to succeed. How much does your passion mean to you? Enough for you to give up all the other lives you could be living, all the other *you's* you could be? Leaving the doors open only provides opportunity for an escape route; nothing ever comes in through this kind of open door.

There's nothing half-hearted about success and no half-hearted performer ever got it. You can't have everything; *have something*. You can't be everywhere; *be somewhere*. You can't be everyone; *be someone*. Life is a choice; *choose one*.

Don't miss out on your life in an effort not to miss out on your life.

Everything you imagine "total involvement" to be is an illusion, an imaginary place created by your seat on the fence. The truth is you don't know what your passion will offer you once you allow yourself to be there, to be completely involved, to close those other doors and be you. The real prize is saved for those willing to take the risk that being *here* entails. Success is one of those prizes.

ONE OF THEM

So too, getting off the fence is about becoming part of something bigger than yourself, part of an "us." True involvement demands that you be willing to render your passion as "worthy" of belonging to. An opera singer in a conversation with herself:

> *The performance was spectacular; the applause for my solo, unbelievable. I sang brilliantly and felt utterly included, celebrated and respected. It was a night of total involvement to which my mind responded with a tornado of self-destruction. 'So now you're one of those people?' my mind mocked me. 'You're one of those people who sings archaic Italian songs? This is the way you've chosen to spend your life?'*

> *Yes, as a matter of fact, I am one of those people, and more appropriately, I am one of an us. And yes, (dare I say it), being part of an us means that I am. Is an identity so dangerous? Must I now be the shooting gallery duck who is paused at the front of the line? Is not zero identity a far worse danger? In holding every group out as a those, am I not clinging fearfully to a*

veil of superiority. Being too good to join a those is simply my way of keeping myself from becoming involved in anything, of refusing to step into and really live my own life. Am I afraid that defining myself will give me an outline and thus make me an easy target? Perhaps the fear is for what I will have to do differently once I choose and settle into an identity, and what my own responsibility will be for that choice. If I am this, then surely I will have to start taking this (as well as myself) seriously. Do I know how to do that?

The old voices speak loudly. How dare you have a life, be part of something! How dare you release your separating, judging, unable-to-be-in-anything mind. To those voices I say, I am *in the opera,* I am *an opera singer,* I am *someone who wants to spend her nights singing old Italian songs. Yes is my answer, I am one of those people. And through that choice, in the bigger picture, so too am I.*

To be fully involved is to become part of a profession and community instead of a perpetual visitor. It is to become a member, an insider. To do so is to give up your comfortable spot on the fence from which you point at and ridicule those who are, shamefully, part of something. Being involved is about humbling yourself enough to say that you are *like* and not better than any group that could possibly exist. By maintaining the illusion of superiority, you *think* you are protecting yourself from the humiliation that is linked to involvement. If you are not one of them, you can't be defined and thus targeted or made fun of. The fault in this logic is that it is only *you* who is making fun of *them*. You are in charge of both the mocking of them and the not-like-them distancing that must follow.

Although you imagine that being part of nothing keeps you safe, this stance, in fact, is quite dangerous. You cannot truly be part of your passion without being part of its "us." Your passion will not avail itself to you until *you* can embrace yourself within it. Passion itself has its own way of sensing those who are not willing or ready to be fully involved. It will wait until the day when you are willing to honor it before honoring *you* with insider's status and/or success. In short, you will not actualize your potential or be treated or feel like a real contender until you accept that your passion *is* who you are.

Can you admit that you *want* to be there? Can you admit to your own interest and ambition? It can be a dangerous thing to admit that you care about something. Caring implies that you can be hurt and disappointed. But caring also means that you can experience the joy and rewards of your effort. Rest assured, nothing can be experienced in the dead zone of chronic ambivalence.

Ironically, once you accept and acknowledge your passion, the possibility of being humiliated for it disappears. It is from the outside that the inside looks so dangerous. Straddling the fence, the ground looks very threatening. What you can't see from where you are however, is the danger that all that "safety" is creating for you. The decision to remain forever undecided puts you at great risk for a far worse punishment, namely, *nothing*. Dying will be the event of your life. Are you willing to make that choice?

By defining yourself, accepting that this *is* who you are, you take on the safety and power of the group, the "us" you are trying so hard not to join. It is within this very "us" (and the identity that it offers) that true protection lays. When you allow yourself to be involved, you step not only into the power of that group, but into the strength of your *own* choice. You immerse yourself in the power that exists in honoring your own identity and the solidness of that definition. When you can do this, you no longer have to fear your own ridicule since you no longer agree with the ridiculer.

3

BEING PRESENT: LEARNING TO PAY ATTENTION

*Attend to the moment;
there is nothing else that matters or exists.
A task well done always brings the right rewards.
The best way to achieve your future
is to achieve your present.*

ATTENTION

*O*nce you have committed to changing, the question arises: What needs to change in order to access your full potential?

"Focus is not my problem," Sarah, an up-and-coming tennis prodigy, reported on her first visit to my office. "I have great concentration during the matches. I just don't understand why I'm not winning because I definitely have the physical skill."

"What specifically are you focusing on or thinking about while you're playing?" I asked.

"I think about how I'm the best player, how I want to do well, show my coach that I know what I'm doing. I guess too, how other people will think I'm playing, whether they'll think I'm really good." Without even realizing it, Sarah had easily given away her problem. She was focused all right, but focused on *what*? She was busy thinking about the result of her match and not the match itself. Nowhere in her response (or her attention) were the individual shots or points she was playing. Nowhere was the tennis.

The most important tool you have is your own attention. And yes, attention *is* a tool. You will reach your personal best when you develop the ability to focus your full attention on this instant, *right now*. Those who can do this one thing can get anywhere. Your work is in learning to be totally present and attentive to the particular task in front of you, to put your attention in the moment and *not* to think about something that happened in the past or what might happen in the future. Each moment is an entirely isolated event with *no* past or future. The only thing that matters is what you need to do in this moment. Greatness demands an understanding and appreciation for the potential of right now. Feel the power of this instant and comprehend that right now is both all there is and everything that matters.

Learning to control your own attention is a skill that must be practiced. Become aware of where your attention is directed at any given moment; know precisely where your mind is residing. Peak performance is about *not* being distracted. It's about concentrating on just one thing—*just the task itself*—not what it will bring, who's watching or how you will look doing it. If you perform your task correctly, all else will take care of itself. Your task is the only thing *you* can control. Success is nothing other than a by-product of completing your task correctly. To focus on your task is to bring your full attention to those specific things you need to *do* to make your performance a great one. A coach who merely tells you to "Go in and win it" is an ignorant coach. By directing your attention to winning, he is putting your focus on the future, thereby, distracting you from the present moment and your task at hand. The emphasis has moved from the process itself to the result. Such a coach is dispersing your focus and energy, weakening your most powerful tool. Winning takes place in the future; your performance takes place right now. You must first be fully here in the right now before anything can happen in your future.

THE PRESENT

Being present means learning to notice and work with the state your body is in at this moment and developing the flexibility to work with changing conditions. Successful performers are not necessarily more physically talented, but they always have more skill at reacting to what is actually happening. For winning performers, success is dependent upon having a repertoire of skills that can handle whatever "present" emerges.

Some days you will be "on" and your body will move better than it does on other days. Sometimes the conditions will favor you, other times not. The trick is to keep focusing your attention on what *is* happening and not waste it lamenting what is *not* or what *should* be. If you can't address what is, you can't make it better. In a performance of any kind, you must be able to accept your right now in whatever form it arrives, attending and adjusting with your full attention and energy. Greatness can only occur in the right now!

From a session with a rider:

Something very positive happened today. I won despite never being fully in the zone. I was not able to reach that place where everything clicks and feels easy. That's not the good part. What was different and positive was that instead of panicking, I rode through and with what I did have, I remained present in what was. The result: consistency prevailed, without the brilliance, but with its own "nuts and bolts" kind of success. At this week's horse show, consistency was enough to capture the championship. Had I focused my energy on where I wasn't and what my body was not able to do, I would surely have lost. Instead, I chose to work with what was and focus on how I was actually riding in the moment. The result feels almost more satisfying than those times when it's effortless.

WHERE ARE YOU?

The mind's nature is to want to get *out* of this moment, to be anywhere but here. Can you be aware of *not* being here? Can you learn to pay attention to your own distraction? The answer is *yes*, but it takes work and practice. It happens by training yourself to continually "check in" on your own attention. Ask yourself again and again, "Where is my attention? Where am I? Am I here in this moment?" If not, notice where your attention is and gently bring it back to where you are, back to you. Do not be discouraged if most of the time you find that your thoughts are off in the past or future and *not* here with right now, *not* attending to what needs to be done to create your peak performance. When you discover that your mind is elsewhere, be gentle with yourself. This is *not* another opportunity to criticize and destroy yourself. Simply nudge, or if necessary, yank your mind back into right now and the task in front of you. Re-establish your own presence. In most cases, the act of consciously noticing where your attention is will be enough to bring it back to the present. For as long as you've been alive, your mind has been practicing the art of leaving the moment. It's good at it. Don't expect it to be good at staying here, at least not right away. Like the techniques of your craft, being *here* is a skill. Practice it.

DESERVING
SUCCESS

*Why not **you?***
*Why **not** you?*
***Why** not you?*
Why not you!

⁓

THE REAL YOU

Who is the *real* you, the you *you* see when you look in the mirror? Is it the one who wins or the one who struggles along, not getting what she wants? Anne, a concert violinist, explains it this way: "When I play well, it's just a fluke, nothing more. That's not the real me up there." The real Anne (in her mind) is the musician who is disappointed, always grasping for success but never fully living it, always a shade away from greatness. When asked about her successes, she replies, "My successes are just exceptions to the bigger picture of who I really am." No matter how consistently Anne plays, the real her remains locked in this old childhood image.

"Who is the real Anne?" I ask.

"Anne is the one who doesn't deliver when it counts," she says matter-of-factly. Of this she is certain, even as she accepts her third Carnegie Hall invitation.

What is frightening about saying good-bye to this you who doesn't get what she wants? Why do you cling to this image of yourself, recreate her everyday in an effort not to lose her? Despite the suffering she has brought to your life, you are comfortable with her; you know her pain. She is the very fabric of your being. Letting go of her would mean abandoning yourself. Who would you be were you not her? Would you even exist? In truth, she is only who you *think* you are, and more accurately, who you have been programmed to think you are. S*he* is already gone! Clinging to her is abandoning only *today's* you. The capable, present you is she who is being lost and ignored. Why do you resist getting to know the successful you? What would happen were you to expand and evolve your self-image to include her? Instead of a winner who occasionally makes mistakes, why must the *real* you be a loser who perpetually surprises you by succeeding? Why is the real you not allowed to *be* that winner?

Do you deserve to be number one? Do you belong at the top? Feeling that you truly deserve to succeed is the critical element in becoming a winner, the universal quality that exists among those who win. To reach the top you must believe that you can and should be number one.

THE GLOW ON TOP

From a session with Anne in which we explored her resistance to success:

> **Anne:** *If I step into my own success, I've got to trade in my anonymity. I won't be safe anymore. Maybe being average protects me in a way. I suppose I've got to learn to reside in that spotlight as opposed to just visiting it. I don't know if I'm ready for that, all those expectations. So much about that seems out of control...like it's not my place this time around. All I know is I get kind of nervous and excited but definitely nervous when I consider it.*

Are you ready to trade in the safety of the sidelines for the solitary glow of the spotlight? How does this possibility sound to you? Imagine yourself at the top of your craft, just you there on stage, basking in the light of brilliance. How does the adoration feel? Does the attention make you feel guilty? Are you not supposed to be in such a position? Does your success make others feel defeated, your winning make others losers? Can you bear to be treated as someone who is powerful and important? Are you supposed to be a "good girl" and make room for the others, not take up so much space for yourself? Or does the whole idea of being the star seem too unreal to imagine, something that could never happen in your *real* life? Is it not your destiny to be a winner?

Left unchecked, the belief that you shouldn't be or don't belong on top will eat away at your foundation like worms under your feet, restricting and destroying any success you accomplish. No matter how hard you work, the feeling that you are not deserving of the spotlight will cause your feet to slip on the rotten footing that is your mind. None of it will happen until *you* believe that you have the right to be the star. Being number one means accepting that you deserve to live a glorious life, to be recognized for who you are, which includes your skill, hard work, passion and everything else that is you.

Why are you attached to a frustrated, struggling, disappointed you? How do you feel about this you? Do you feel sorry for her? Hate her? Are you embarrassed by her? Who relates to you as *her*? Is this your *family's* daughter? Who does *her* presence keep alive? What relationships does *she* make possible? Now just for a moment, imagine the real you as a star. Who is this you? What does she look like? How is she different from the old version of you? What are the positive and negative feelings you have for *her*? How does she relate to those in your past? Is she threatening, intimidating, too powerful? With whom would this successful and deserving you surround herself? With whom would she dispense? If she would, why won't you? Whom or what would you lose if you were to let yourself be *this* you? In truth, have you already become this you?

WHAT ABOUT YOU?

Continue asking yourself the same question, "Why not me?" Ask your heart as well as your head. Do you deserve to be punished for something you've done or perhaps something you are? Are you inherently unworthy as a human being? What is your failing? Why are you not allowed to be the one at the top? Why don't you deserve a glorious life? Relief, however, does not come with just understanding. Relief and change come when you can develop compassion for that part of you that feels so undeserving. Can you feel the suffering of this undeserving self, the pain that this overwhelming self-doubt has caused in your life? It is nothing less than tragic to have lived your life feeling that you don't deserve success, convinced that the winner's circle is a place for others but not you. How much (and what specifically) have you lost in your life because of these beliefs? How hard has it been for you to accomplish anything with this not-for-me mentality? Allow yourself to experience what you have lost.

What does it feel like to say "Why not me?" Can you really mean it? Force yourself to stay with the question until you generate some outrage for the way you've treated yourself. Feel what it feels like to make a demand, if only from yourself. Those who succeed can envision themselves as successful. And most of all, they know they deserve it.

GOOD JOB

How do you handle praise? Do you react by correcting the one praising you and highlighting everything you did wrong? Do you attempt to dissuade others from admiring you? Are you comfortable pointing out other people's strengths but self-conscious or embarrassed when talking about your own? Practice talking about yourself and YOUR accomplishments. Make an effort to listen to the praise you are offered; force yourself to respond with a simple "Thank you." Become aware of how desperately you want to make a rebuttal, how difficult it is for you to let yourself shine. Refrain from trying to convince the world that you don't deserve to be recognized. By allowing a positive vision of yourself to go unchallenged, you take a step toward developing a new vision of yourself. At the very least, you make a positive self-image a *possibility*.

In each of your performances there will be flaws that only you notice. Because you are the one actually performing, certain information and sensations are available only to you. Praise does not imply that you have duped your audience into thinking that you were perfect. You may indeed have succeeded at concealing the difficulties you faced in your performance. On the other hand, your audience may be complimenting you on precisely your ability to handle such problems. Either way, it is only you who expects perfection from yourself and your performance. In your eyes, the fact that difficulties arose at all makes you imperfect, and therefore, all praise invalid. Your imperfection nullifies any compliment that might come your way, making you responsible only for fooling your audience.

From an inside perspective, there is no such thing as a perfect performance. The very nature of being inside something makes it imperfect. No matter who you are, there is always room to be better. Expecting your performances to be problem-free is a childish fantasy. Being a professional means accepting problems as a part of the game and making an effort to work with them. The presence of difficulty has nothing to do with the existence of talent. Perfection exists only within the context of imperfection. Learning to recognize and honor your own talent in the midst of this imperfection is an important task.

SABOTAGE

What role are you playing in your own success? Are you the chink in the armor, the thing that has to be "gotten around" in order for that success to happen? If so, success is something that can only happen *despite* you or *without* your awareness. In truth, it is not *in spite* of you that you achieve but *because* of you. Your potential will be reached not as a result of your absence, but rather, your presence. Can you trust yourself? Is your own presence a positive force? Do you walk onto the stage knowing that you will play on your own team? Or, sadly, is your goal to simply get through the performance without sabotaging yourself? Is the majority of your energy devoted to simply keeping your self-destructive impulses at bay?

For Janet, a singer, the biggest problem on stage was herself. While performing, she lived in constant fear of that self and what it would do to her. She felt that her most basic instincts were self-destructive, that she was always seeking to ruin what she had accomplished, "If I sing one passage well, I am sure to clutch in the next. It is once I become conscious of singing well that my luck inevitably ends." Having to monitor and control her self-destroying aspect drained Janet of her energy and distracted her attention from her task on stage. She could not be fully in her experience while trying to keep her destructive instincts in check. There simply wasn't enough attention or energy to do both well. In order to perform at the top level, she needed to utilize all of herself, to be able to turn her full attention to the music. As it stood, only a small slice of her attention was actually focused on the task of singing; the rest of her was either looking for the opportunity to destroy or restrain that very instinct. In either case, a big part of her was missing. As she put it, "I've got so much going on and so very little of it has anything to do with my song. Can you imagine how I would sing if *all* of me were performing at one time? I couldn't fail; I would be unstoppable."

For Janet, the task was not in developing *stronger* tactics with which to combat her self-sabotage, but just the opposite. Self-sabotage is not something you can kill; it will kill you first. It is the way Janet had been addressing her self-sabotage that had allowed it to stick around for so long. Mistakenly, she had been feeding it when she thought she was controlling it. There is *never* enough talent to compensate for being your own enemy. The very act of waging war against your self-sabotaging instincts contributes to those self-destructive tendencies. The self-sabotaging instinct responds to your attempts to force it into submission by getting stronger, robbing more of your energy, demanding more of your attention and thus feeding the very beast you are fighting. The message you send yourself is that *you* must be suppressed in order to get anything done. How welcome and appreciated could that *you* then feel? Why would you want to work for her happiness? She is the enemy! It is only through developing a sense of kindness toward yourself that you will actually lose the urge to destroy your own success. Mind you, your kindness can not be reserved for just the spectacular, confident and likable you but must extend to the insecure, competitive, mean-spirited, greedy and whatever other you's exist. The compassion is for *all* of you and particularly, the you who has suffered so intensely and lost so much at the work of your own hands.

The idea of letting your guard down can sound very threatening. Surely this would leave you free to thoroughly destroy yourself. Certain that *you* must be watched like a hawk, the instinct is to initiate more restriction, harsher rules, keep a tighter hold on yourself. The more intense the possibility of sabotage, the stronger the systems you must have in place to fight yourself. And ready, you must always be. Caring about yourself could only mean one thing: chaos. But punishment and control will not work. Has it worked so far? Has it relieved the burden of having to monitor and suppress your own instincts? Has it helped you get where and what you want, made you feel differently about yourself?

Why don't you deserve to get what you want? This is, after all, what you are saying when you commit sabotage. Loud and clear, you are confirming that you see yourself as someone who should have her happiness taken away, who should *not* get what she wants. Addressing just the self-sabotaging behavior itself does nothing to make you feel any different about this self whose happiness you are trying so hard to destroy. The only way to stop the sabotage is to stop seeing and treating yourself as someone who deserves to be sabotaged. If you don't like this self or don't think she deserves to be happy, you will forever find a way to block her success. Rather than attempting to curtail the sabotaging behavior, it is your feelings about yourself that must change. You must truly want to *help* this self (*your* self), to stop *wanting* to ruin your chance at happiness in order for the sabotage to finally end.

ARE YOU READY TO TRY SOMETHING NEW?

Would you try and destroy the happiness of someone you loved? Or conversely, would you do whatever you could to help this someone get what she wanted? This is the point: *you* must become someone you love! *You* must become someone whom you believe deserves to be happy! This is not a task of strength; you can not bully yourself into playing on your own team (or caring about yourself for that matter). The only way "out" is by going in—softness for you in place of strength against you. The only way you can count on your own presence on the stage is if that presence sincerely wants to help you.

STOP RIGHT NOW! Notice your thoughts at this second. What are you thinking as you read this? Have you already turned this into an intellectual pursuit, one that you're not really going to *apply* to your life? Are you thinking that this might work for other people but you can't (and don't want to) learn how to be kind or soft (or any of those other "weak" emotions) when it comes to yourself. (Are you saying inside that this will never work with you—that this writer doesn't know the power of your mind!) Notice how quickly and completely you can reject the possibility of something new for yourself. For others, maybe, but not for you. Humor me. Just for a moment, assume that I do know the power of your mind. Just for a moment, suspend your judgments and put your big toe in the water. Just for a moment, go towards your fear instead of away from it. Assume that you too can change, you too can learn to be gentle with yourself, you too can learn to succeed. How much do you want to change? If you want to experience change you have to be willing to *do* the scratching and crawling that goes into carving out a new system of living. You have to try something *new*, become something *new*. *You* have to do it, no one else can do it for you! *You* have to be willing to enter the unknown, to surrender your doubt, to try something that you do not understand. You can live an entirely different kind of life, but first you must let the possibility for that life exist.

How much of your suffering is by your own doing? How much have you endured as a result of your own punishment? What might it feel like to find encouragement and comfort in your own presence? What if you were to *want* it to be *you* at the plate with the bases loaded? How would it feel if, without controlling it, you could count on yourself to do what was *best* for you? What could you accomplish if all of your talent and energy were working in your favor? Would *you* too be unstoppable? When you care about you, you are free to turn your full attention to your task, confident that the unchaperoned and unshackled you can be trusted.

So how do you do this, you wonder, this thing called being gentle with yourself, this new life? How do you put an end to the constant punishment and control of your own spirit? The first step is awareness, simply recognizing the extent of your own suffering. What has it really been like to live inside your mind, your body, your soul? Before reading on, explore this question on your own. Start a journal and write about just this question. No one else needs to hear your answers. It is an exercise just for you. The feelings that this question evokes are the beginning of a new kind of life.

IMPERFECTION

Accept imperfection and you are free to approach perfection.
When you remove "should," you discover "can."
Can you allow yourself to learn?

⁓

Nikki at 22 is an accomplished swimmer and a self-described perfectionist "to the nth degree." For Nikki, it is her internal audience that creates the problems. "Certainly I am embarrassed when others have witnessed my imperfection, but it's nothing like the humiliation I feel in front of myself." With each failure, she attacks herself more viciously, with labels from "mediocre" to "absurd," reeling in self-hatred beneath their weight. "Being in the middle of the pack (which of course my mistake implies) levels me to a state of nothingness. My concern is not that others are whispering about my error; it is me who is shouting at myself for being less than perfect. I am sickened by my own imperfection."

"What is the worst thing about your imperfection?" I ask. "What's there in the center of your humiliation?"

"During these times when I am not protected by perfection, the worst thing, the thing I am most afraid of is being with myself. I know that my internal audience will soon devour me. My mistake destroys everything good about me, all of my skill and anything positive I created in the midst of the mistake. The mistake acts like a bulldozer, leveling and wiping out all good things that came before it. I imagine that my mistake confirms that I am not a contender, not a serious competitor. The error has proven (to my audience and myself) that I will never be able to claim the top spot, and that underneath it all, I am no more than average and certainly not a player bound for greatness. My mistake proves that I am a 'clutcher,' an athlete who can *never* come through when it counts."

PROCESS NOT OUTCOME

Unfortunately for Nikki, it is the very presence of her mistake that defines it as a time that "counts." Because she "failed," it "counted." For this talented athlete, imperfection is synonymous with being a loser. As she put it (contemptuously), "Let's be honest, you can't be a winner and make mistakes. Some facts are just facts." As you can see, there is a very small window within which Nikki can maintain a feeling of legitimacy. She is like a trapeze artist who must practice without a net; each minor mistake results in a life-threatening injury. Nikki may sound like an extreme example, but she is completely ordinary when it comes to the injury performers inflict upon themselves for the sin of imperfection.

Imperfection

How do you feel about yourself when you make a mistake? How do you define or re-define yourself in the face of imperfection? How would you describe the imperfect you? How do you talk to her? Does a mistake send you plunging into self-hatred, create feelings of despair and worthlessness? Are you humiliated when the truth about your being human is revealed? What does it mean for you to *not* be perfect? For very competitive people, the hardest skill to learn is how to forgive themselves for not being perfect. Do you know how to forgive yourself?

Putting an end to mistake-induced devastation begins by accepting the idea of process. You are involved in a process, the process of becoming an expert, the process that is your craft. Even after you have gotten "there" (wherever it is you think you are heading), you will continue to make mistakes. Deciding to be great means agreeing to be in the process of learning; making mistakes *is* learning. Mistakes stop happening when you are finished. You are *never* finished. There is no end, no point at which the learning stops. Your passion is the process; it is the race and *not* the finish line. There are certain things that you must learn over and over again; this too is part of the process. You have chosen to be *here* in the game, this place where the mistakes and the learning goes on. Your mistakes, like your victories, are all part of this process that is your passion. The good parts are as much *it* as the bad. You must learn to appreciate and accept *all* of its parts. This is not to say that when you make an error you are happy or that the defeats are as enjoyable as the victories. They are not. Not wanting to make mistakes is a good thing, but committing yourself to greatness means making the decision to be *in* your passion for the long haul, to take it on with *all* of its parts. Who told you it was going to be easy? *It's not supposed to be easy*. You imagine that it's supposed to be fun and easy all the time. This is not the case with passion. Greatness includes hardship, *always*. The hardship is as much a part of, and as important as, the success and joy. Learn to *love* it even in those moments when you are *hating* it. Your agony comes from expecting that it should be different, that your passion is supposed to include only good times, that the passion *is* the fun part while the difficult times are something separate, something to outgrow. Wrong. Just as you cannot develop self-love while separating and rejecting those aspects of yourself you don't like, so too your passion is a whole that must be accepted and appreciated for all of its parts.

Mistakes are opportunities, a signal that it's time to learn. As far-fetched as it may seem, you must appreciate your errors as the teachers that they are. Your mistakes are not humiliations but just the opposite, messengers sent to make you even better, to lead you one step further down the road of excellence. Excellence is a road and not a destination. By hating your mistakes and yourself for committing them, you are childishly demanding to appear as an expert without wanting to actually know more or be better. Passion is not about getting through the process while appearing perfect. If that were the case, the goal would be to hurry up and die perfect, to get out of the game while your record was still clean. Do you want to really know your craft? Do you want to actually improve? Do you want to be great because you love it? If the answer is yes, then mistakes are your allies. Your insistence on perfection is the real enemy.

BEING LOST

"There are times when I lose everything, when I feel like a complete beginner who knows nothing at all about swimming, this thing I'm *supposed* to be so good at. I hate myself during these stretches...I feel totally child-like and silly, like I have no right to be here, like it's all a big fat waste of time. It's during these times when I can't do anything right that it's like proof that I'm still not a legitimate athlete. These are the times when it's really hard to justify staying in it and not hanging the whole thing up. I guess I don't trust that it's ever going to end, like I'll ever be able to do it right again."

Unfortunately, Nikki has it backwards. In truth, it is the immature performer who abandons the "journey into knowing nothing," the path to "Beginnersville." The undeveloped performer must run from the fear imposed by such periods in order to re-confirm her legitimacy, to escape the darkness and self-loathing that such "lostness" inspires. These jaunts into the unknown, where Nikki questions every ounce of her talent, these are the very tests of her legitimacy. It is the seasoned, legitimate performer who can tolerate and trust such periods of understanding *nothing*, feeling utterly helpless and ignorant, such times when she is sure that all of her work has been for naught and that she will never know anything again. What Nikki doesn't trust is that the not knowing is simply part of the process of knowing and therefore, of all learning.

Greatness does not come easy (or hadn't you noticed). Those who can tolerate the darkness (and it may prove to be that of an Alaskan winter), know that the light will return. You will find your way back to the path of knowing. And most importantly, when you get back there you will not be in the same place as where you started! Remind yourself again and again: it is precisely your ability and willingness to weather the "lostness" that defines your right to be on the journey. No matter how far along you are on your particular path, you will never cease in revisiting Beginnersville. As long as you are striving, you can count on being back there. And yet, despite knowing this you may still choose to thrash about and hate yourself each time you find yourself back there, to call yourself every nasty name you can think of for being where you are. Such a struggle is unnecessary but none-the-less it is *your* energy, your choice of how to use or waste it. Regardless of how you react however, do not lose sight of the meaning (and privilege) of being part of a process that has its own logic. The stretches of blind wandering are as much a part of the road of excellence as are the periods when you feel your feet solidly on firm ground—strongly defined, rewarded and with a direction that is clear. When all touch with that direction (and those feet) is lost, you are simply in another part of the same process. Trust that process to lead you home again. In the end, true experts are always the best beginners.

THE MYTH OF PERFECTION

A quick note on perfection: it doesn't exist. It is in fact, nothing more than a gilded cage, a trap. *Mistakes are part of the game.* The sooner you figure out how to work with them instead of trying to make them go away, the sooner you, too, will be one of the great ones.

Being afraid to make mistakes creates them. If you can't make mistakes, you can't try new things. If you can't try new things, you can't get better. If you can't get better, you can't become great. Your obsession with perfection stunts your growth. It forces you to steer away from anything that might lead to failure and *that* means anything new or unknown. With perfection as your overriding goal, you are confined to stagnation. The process of brilliance is one of climbing and falling. When the falling stops, so does the climbing. Each time you fail, you have carved out a place in which to improve and grow. You have planted the seed for a new tree. The need for perfection forces you to play within the safe zone, with those techniques that you know won't fail you. This is not to say that there isn't a place for this kind of safe-play in certain performances, but training is different. There is no place for perfection in training. You must allow yourself to make mistakes while working. It is in the mistakes that new things develop and true brilliance arises. You cannot know where a mistake will take you, how it will help or where it will eventually lead your performance.

Excellence demands that you be willing to stomach this unknown, to make a beginner out of yourself, to let this unknown into your training, to trust that your mistakes will guide you to a place that you can't know from where you are. How much are you willing to risk for your passion? How uncomfortable are you willing to feel? What if you were to shift your perspective on the unknown? Instead of something there to hurt you, what if you were to see it as your friend, one who asks for your hand so that she may lead you to a more expansive place. You must offer your own hand in return before this unknown warrior will lead you to your next peak. Consider the process of mating. Your system insists that you reach the comfort and love of marriage without having to first stumble through the process of dating. If on your first date you don't have the feeling that you want to have on your tenth wedding anniversary, you're ready to throw in the towel. Using only what you know gets boring. If those things you already know were all you needed, wouldn't you already be number one? Are you ready for something new? If you answered yes, then it's time for the big three: imperfection, learning and brilliance (in that order). You're imperfect. Get over it and start getting *great*.

THE FIX

After having committed an error, Nikki's tendency was to want to get away from her mistake, to run and hide from the imperfection that now defined her, to escape the state of not knowing that created so much discomfort and humiliation. "It's all about my left shoulder," she said, trying to convince me along with herself. "When I can rotate it a tiny bit farther I'll pick up the seconds. It's just a matter of my going to the gym more often and strengthening that rhomboid." The cold truth was, neither she nor her coach knew why her times were getting slower. Nikki felt helpless. Enter the magic bullet (her left shoulder rotation). Designing an immediate "answer" to her problem gave Nikki back the illusion of control in a situation that felt totally out of control. So too, she felt less humiliated once she had determined exactly what the problem was. As long as she knew what it was, she wasn't helpless, she could fix it. And if she could fix it, there was no reason to feel humiliated. As you can see, a lot of birds get killed with just one bullet!

The problem with the magic bullet approach is multi-layered. To begin with, today's solution may fix today's problem, but soon the problem will mutate. When it does, you will once again feel helpless and out of control. Today's problem will come in exactly today's disguise just this once. Your post-mortem solution will not apply to tomorrow's version of the same problem. This is not to say that you should cease trying to correct your errors, but the process is more involved than just slapping on a quick fix. This fix may temporarily relieve the stress of not knowing, but it is a case of applying a Band-Aid when what you need to do is strengthen your immune system. Today's bullet calms the anxiety generated by your imperfection, and yet the longer you compete, the less relief you will find in this solution-of-the-moment. No matter how hard you try to convince yourself, deep down you know that both the problem and the solution are bigger than your magic bullet. If they weren't, you would have solved it long ago.

Hitting the problem with a magic bullet calms your anxiety by taking you from an unknown situation into one that is known, from your out-of-control imperfection to a state of control and the renewed delusion of possible perfection. Unfortunately, this approach limits your ability to truly grow out of the problem. This quick fix is something that you already know, and it is precisely why it was available to you so immediately. The fact that you made the error implies that you *do not* yet know the answer. You are groping for a solution out of what you already know, the very pool of knowledge that led you to your current predicament. You must be able to sit with the feeling of not yet being able to do it right. You may have to play without the solution for some time before you figure it out. The magic bullet is created to lessen your anxiety and close off the not knowing. In your rush to get away from the mistake and out of this unknown, however, you also shut out the potential for real learning, forego the incredible opportunity that your error offers. Your fix-it solution closes the door to any discovery of what the real problem is. Your "answer" puts an iron fence around an unknowable space, restricting new ideas from entering the field while prohibiting the possibility for expansion. When you build a fence made of stale knowledge you destroy the opportunity for real improvement. The unknown is the only soil for true growth.

From an athlete's journal:

My self-hatred stems from my inability to accept a self who doesn't know everything and is imperfect. I feel destroyed by my failure to control the situation. As long as I am afraid to sit with my weaker parts, my fallibility, these parts will continue to rule me. The magic bullet serves as paltry protection from the vast repertoire of errors that exists within me. The unknown must become an acceptable place to be and have within me. I may never actually choose to reside in this unknown, but I must learn to approach the "not knowing" as a place where I can learn and be (as opposed to one that destroys me).

Even if I do manage to tame today's mistake by whispering the right phrase to myself, sooner or later today's word will lose its power. I will then be back in the hell where I am now. It is the self-hatred that results from my imperfection that I must correct, even more than the problems themselves. Rushing to fix the problem without trying to genuinely improve only encourages my perfect-or-nothing mentality.

The magic bullet approach has yet another downside.

In continually reminding herself of what needs to be done (or how *not* to screw it up), Nikki was confirming that her instincts could not be trusted. "But they *can't* be trusted," she would say, "just look at my record." One thing was sure, she would never know if they could by doubting them from the outset. "But I tried trusting them and they failed me. I did it wrong," she barked, frustrated by the idea that she might be able to believe in herself.

"Fine," Nikki smirked combatively. "Today I'm going to do whatever my instincts tell me. If all goes well, I'll trust them and you forever. Whatever you tell me to do, I'll do. Whatever I have a hunch about, I'll go with. On the other hand, if it doesn't work out today, I'll know I can never trust my instincts again." Rest assured, *this* is not trusting your instincts. *This* is dragging a bruised and battered horse from the stall where he has sat for years, never being given the chance to run or feel the sun, opening the gate and expecting him to come out and win the Kentucky Derby. The instincts that you are "respecting" in these trials are already "disrespected," regardless of how you re-label them for the day. At their core, they are distrusted, *you* are distrusted. The process must be a deeper one, of learning to respect yourself and thus the judgment that comes out of that self regardless of whether it leads to mistakes or not.

LEARNING

Learning requires one thing: the ability to say I don't know. If not to anyone else, at least to yourself. It requires that you admit to your own patches of ignorance as well as your desire to know more. Are you overwhelmed or frightened by this state of not knowing? Does not knowing leave you feeling exposed and in danger of criticism? Being great at anything is a direct result of courage, and specifically, the courage to *learn*. Your needing and wanting to learn should by no means be grounds for humiliation—just the opposite, self-respect. By giving yourself permission to learn, you are expressing your willingness to go into the unknown, to risk giving up your comfortable place of knowing in an effort to grow and expand.

Learning is actually quite simple; it is the direct result of being able to say "I don't know." "I don't know" is the most powerful sentence you will ever utter. There are no three words that hold more opportunity or potential than these. How do you *feel* when you say these words? Is it an "admission" for you? How do you feel when learning something new? Threatened? Excited? Humbled? Frightened? Humiliated? Energized? The question is *not* what you think about learning. To that, I'm sure you have a compassionate and intellectual response. But rather, how do you feel when in the process of learning, when faced with something you don't yet understand?

Although you may think you are protecting yourself, refusing to take the risk that comes with learning imprisons your potential. *It keeps you stuck.* Pretending you know everything prevents you from learning anything. You are thus prohibited from developing and becoming a *true* expert. You can *look* like an expert in your safe cave, but you will never *be* an expert as long as the world outside that cave is off-limits. With your own curiosity as your enemy, too humiliating or terrifying to approach, you remain a prisoner of your tiny, finite universe. Although you may convince yourself that you are the master of your comfortable little cave, in truth, you are nothing more than a slave to it.

In order to become truly powerful, a *true* expert, you must give up your imagined fiefdom and become an ordinary man in the land of questions. The opportunity to not know brings incredible freedom. Suddenly, you are there to learn, not expecting yourself to know everything, open to the possibility of expanding without judging yourself for not already *being* the expert you want to become. Remember, you've got to *become* that expert, that's the only way it can happen. And remember too, there is plenty that *that* expert doesn't know as well. Take the shackles off—*allow* yourself to learn and grow. The courage to live in the unknown is the prerequisite for greatness.

Many performers want to disown their past, disclaim their earlier stages when they knew less. But what if you were to award the *more* experienced *you* the very same power you do this earlier version of yourself? What if you chose to see the present as a fresh place *made possible* through past experience? Can you award the same power to your present as you do your past? The performer you were, the one who knew less than you do today, "she" is your ally. Your current knowledge is built on top of hers; "she" is *your* foundation, the legs on which you now play. Without her, you would be a tree with no roots. Can you be proud of her? Can you give her credit for growing? After all, she grew into *you*. Be proud of *today's* you; you *became* this performer, this person you are today. You *earned* it. To think it could happen any other way is like expecting yourself to be able to run without ever having walked (I won't mention crawl). Both your past and the *you* who lived it got you to who and where you are now. This past *you* was your teacher; all that you now understand is because of her. She remains in your care; she belongs to you. You can't honor the present *you* while rejecting and disowning your past. Until you can accept the performer you *were*, you can't be the performer you are or *want to be*.

ACCEPTANCE

To accept *yourself* as imperfect is *not* the same thing as labeling your problems as "acceptable." The problems are not acceptable, *you* are. It is this *self*-acceptance that gives you the freedom to address the situation, that throws open the door to true exploration and growth. Once you are OK with being less-than-perfect, you can really get to work within that imperfect space. When you offer yourself the permission (and freedom) to be imperfect, you give yourself the space to become a better performer. As a result, accepting yourself as imperfect is, ironically, what leads you to genuinely trusting yourself. It is only the imperfect you whom you can trust to create greatness.

Recovering from the devastation that mistakes induce is about developing a sense of compassion for the you who made that bad decision or flawed move. It is easy to feel kindness for the you who is here now, the you who knows it was a bad decision, the you who would do it differently if given the chance. The work is in learning to accept this *other* you, this fallible, incorrect decision maker. She is the one who you must learn to love, even in her ignorance. The you who had the wrong answer, who didn't know enough, didn't have enough experience to make the right decision or move. This is who *you* were when you made the mistake. No matter who you are capable of being now, the very fact that this was who you were in that moment means that there was no one else you could have been and nothing more that you could have done. The very fact that you chose to do what you did in that moment means that it was the *best* that you could do in that moment (although maybe not your best ever or even the previous moment's best). When you can accept what you were doing that moment, and that *you's* best, you will then be free to move on. "I was just being lazy when I did it." "I knew it was the wrong decision then." "It *wasn't* my real best." "I'm much better than that." I've heard your arguments. All of them may be true to a certain extent, but remember, if you could have done it differently in that moment, you would have. If it was just you "being lazy" then *you* were a lazy person in that moment. Your laziness is a part of you—it cannot be separated from who *you* are. In your system, the *real* and *only* you is the perfect you, the you you approve of. Anything other than that represents someone who isn't really you. In fact, the you who is strong and alert (and always makes the right decision) is only one of many you's. Put yourself back in the shoes of the you who made that wrong decision; she is you as well. Don't turn your back on her. Rather, feel what she was feeling when she made that decision. Try and understand her process. She was, after all, doing the best that she could do in that moment, even if she didn't live up to your expectations.

In your mind, everyone is out there pointing at your mistake, laughing at you. Convinced that the error is all that's visible in your performance, the mistake erases everything you did right. Either you are perfect or utterly worthless—there's no in-between. The presence of an error destroys your chances of being a real competitor since everyone knows that real competitors don't make errors. For you, a mistake is the drop of ink that discolors the entire glass of water. In truth, a mistake is more like a dime dropped into that same glass, a small entity amidst the larger substance. In reality, the coin does not contaminate or affect the rest of the water; the two co-exist, each retaining their substance and size.

Real performers make mistakes. The better the performer, the harder it is to see their mistakes. The goal is not to get to a place where mistakes cease to exist; if this were the case you would always be a failure as mistakes are *always* going to be a part of the process. The real goal in performance is learning to conceal the problems that do occur while continually solving them and moving on to new problems. The mistakes themselves never go away. They are part of the process called excellence. What must end however, is the expectation that perfection will ever be reached. Top performers accept error as part of the performance process and not something that must or ever will be eliminated.

SHOULD: THE WORST OF ALL WORDS

When you fixate on your past mistakes, you are focusing on what *should* be as opposed to what *is*. Self-flagellation will not change you into the performer who can do it right. What you can do is change your feeling about the performer who did it wrong and turn your attention to how you want to do it next time. Don't waste your time beating yourself up, yelling at yourself for not being able to do it right, or questioning why you're so pathetic and unable to get the job done. All of this does just one thing, it distracts you from the only moment that matters, the one right now in which you don't yet know how to do it. You're so busy obsessing about what should be and who you're *not* that you have no energy or attention to devote to correcting the actual problem.

Your "why can't I do it like that, be like that" thinking serves a purpose; it allows you to re-enter the known. As taxing a "place" as self-loathing may be, it is a familiar spot. It's you fixating on what and where you *should* be while avoiding the difficult and frightening unknown of where you actually are. Notice how often you busy yourself with what should be, with statements that begin with "why can't I." Bring yourself back to the present and what *is* happening. The only way you can get to "there," to what should be, is by first looking at where you are and what *is*. Ask yourself, "What is right now? What do I have to work with?" It is out of your *now* that you will create your *then*. It is from your *what is* that will arise your *should be*. Until you can look at the performer you *are*, you can't become the performer you *want to be*.

GENERALIZATIONS

"I'm worthless," Nikki muttered after reporting her most recent failure in the pool. "*You're* worthless?" I asked, stressing the *you're* and doing my best to look perplexed. I hoped she would catch the giant leap she had just made from what happened in the pool to the value of her existence. No such luck. "Yeah, think about it; all I do is swim and if I can't do that well, then what exactly am I worth?" Nikki is not alone. Generalizing errors is a big problem for performers.

Left unchecked, a simple mistake grows into a gigantic monster. From a less-than-perfect pirouette, high C note, lob shot or ankle rotation, emerges a giant testimony on your inadequacy and failure as a human being. Does your mistake-induced self-hatred spread like a cancer, taking over every aspect of your self-worth? Until she learned to do it herself, again and again I would remind Nikki of what her mistake actually was, what the specific technique was that she did not execute properly, continually separating the mistake from the person she considered herself to be, continually drawing boundaries around the mistake itself.

Tying your performance to your value as a human being is a dangerous habit. You *must* untie these two. *You* are not your performance. Find another way to define yourself, another way to generate self-worth. Self-worth can not depend on a flawless performance or you will forever ride a roller-coaster of despair. There must be a *you* who can walk off that stage as a successful and talented performer (and person), even after having committed mistakes. There is some part of yourself that you must protect and keep sacred regardless of today's particular outcome. And yet, if you still feel inclined to link your self-worth to your performance, at least make it about the process. Tie your self-image to the discipline, hard work and determination that you put into your craft. Get connected to your unsinkable courage and the will that you demonstrate every day in trying to be better. Forget about the result. The result changes every day and says nothing about who you really are. The process, on the other hand, not only remains consistent in its value, but conveys everything about who you really are, both as a performer and a human being.

So what is the purpose of clinging to your mistakes? What image of yourself are you refusing to let go of by broadening your mistakes into giant character issues? How do you respond to other performers when they are less-than-perfect? Do you offer other performers the right to retain *their* value in the wake of imperfection? Does another player's error obliterate her status as a talented performer? And what about as a human being? Are you repulsed by her because she made a mistake? Does *her* error render her worthless and inept? On the flip side, do you view another performer who makes a mistake as one who is talented but has mis-interpreted a particular inflection, mis-hit a specific overhead or committed some other specific error? Do mistakes remain isolated incidents when it comes to others? Is their failure *specific* to the incident at-hand? Do you offer others this privilege while denying it to yourself?

Your mistake begins and ends on the performance field. Leave it there. The ability to leave the problem where it happened (in the past) is a skill of great competitors. This is not to say that great competitors don't examine their mistakes—they do—but they *move on*. Mistakes happen and then they're over. They can not end however, unless *you* will let them end.

MOVING FORWARD

The best way to work with a mistake is to first understand it, to figure out (if possible) what you actually did wrong. Once you are clear on what the actual mistake was, accept yourself (as much as you can) as the imperfect performer who committed the error, remembering that mistakes are *part* of and not a departure from the path of greatness.

Now listen closely. This next step is the most important of all. Whether you have accepted and forgiven yourself or not, you must now *shift your attention* to a positive image, that of your correct performance. Imagine and *see* yourself executing the "move" exactly as you would have liked it to happen. Keep in mind, accepting your mistake does not imply that you're giving up on solving it, just the opposite. After committing a mistake, your mind instinctively wants to stay *in* the problem, to keep focusing your attention on it, rehashing it, recreating it, replaying it, re-anything it to make it have happened differently. The mind wants to return to the scene of the crime and create order and perfection where there is disorder and imperfection. Obsessively, your mind will insist on fixing the error, over and over until it feels it has closed off the unknown and obliterated the existence of your mistake, your existence as an imperfect being. Reliving the mistake will not change or eliminate it. No matter how many different ways you reconstruct the event, you can not eliminate the fact that it happened nor make it come out another way.

It is against every instinct to "move away" from the error, to let it be, to allow it to exist while turning your attention to something else. No matter how uncomfortable and frightening it feels to let go of the obsessive and controlling re-enactment, you must. By re-playing your error again and again, you are not only abusing yourself but damaging your future performances. Although your intent is to figure out and fix the problem, this negative repetition is actually *counter*-productive to your performance. What you are doing is rehearsing and strengthening your mistake, training your body to repeat the very error you are trying to annihilate, encouraging exactly the opposite of what you want to accomplish. You get better at doing it wrong, solidifying the mistake as you instruct your body to repeat it. The longer you focus on the error, the more you encourage it to return.

By focusing on the image of correctness, your mind creates a magnet, thereby drawing your body into its image and inviting your body to create the perfection you envision. Your attention is your most powerful training tool. Where you choose to put it is where you instruct your body to be. It takes faith and courage to become great. Those who become great are willing and brave enough to risk the unknown by continually leaving behind an imperfect past. Your mistakes can leave you only when you will leave them, when you are

Imperfection

willing to move on. Take your mind to where you *want* to be and trust that your body will follow.

NEGATIVE
SELF-TALK

Must you live your present by the rules of the past?
Life's too short not to play on your own team.

～

Negative self-talk is the continual stream of messages our mind sends us regarding our inadequacies, the repetitive tapes that play in our head reminding us of all that we cannot accomplish because of our failings. Negative self-talk is a way of keeping the old image of ourself alive. This internal dialogue is powerful and particularly dangerous because it shapes our interpretation of all events and becomes a distorted lens through which we see the world of the present. The mind is designed to take in and record every event that happens to us, positive or negative. These records then shape our self-image. The problem is that our negative lens forces us to screen out the positive and focus only on what we do wrong or what is done wrong *to* us. We allow ourselves to digest and record only the negative experiences, those that fit with our inadequate self-image. To say the least, we are a cruel and unusually tough editor of our own experience. Our expectations and self-image are thus quite small, given that the only memories logged on the mind's computer are disappointments.

Consider the case of a tennis player named Jamie. Jamie's underlying belief about herself is that she is completely and perpetually average, nothing spectacular. She is convinced that she will never be one of the top players on the tour. Jamie believes that she is talented but not important or special enough to be on top, that it is not her destiny to be in the spotlight. Jamie feels like she is just pretending to be a "real" athlete, that underneath it all she is really an impostor *faking* her expertise. No matter what she accomplishes, she holds to her belief that she is mediocre. In order to support these beliefs about herself, Jamie's inner tapes must play continually throughout her daily experience.

When her coach compliments her on a match, Jamie's internal dialogue runs as follows: "Now I've really fooled him, now I'll have to keep up this level of play or he'll see what a loser I really am. If I screw up now, not only will I be the failure I am, but an athlete who can't stand up to the pressure. I'll be a choker." She reminds herself that other players who win are "real" winners while she could never compete with these players on a serious level. She maintains this belief despite her beating these others as often as she loses to them. Jamie can acknowledge that she plays well occasionally, but in her mind each time is just as much a fluke as the last.

When a lower-ranked player congratulates Jamie on a victory, the following reaction is triggered "She's just congratulating me because it's such a surprise that I won, so out of character for me. If I were a "real" winner, it wouldn't be such a big deal, they would just expect it of me." The praise thus only contributes to Jamie's feelings of humiliation. When Jamie plays well but is defeated, she reminds herself that it is just her destiny to lose. "See," she says, "I can play great tennis and still I can't win. I'm just not meant to be on top." This commentary plays no matter how much success she (in reality) achieves or how consistently things go her way.

Despite a completely different situation, Jamie's inner dialogue is almost identical, at least in purpose. After winning an early round match in a big tournament, she whispers to herself "Now I've used up my one good performance. I'll never be able to play like that again. There's no way that fluke will repeat itself. What's worse is that it *happened* to me early in the tournament. Even if I were able to keep playing decently, the "real" players will be peaking as the matches go on. They will be reaching their stride while I've already used up my best. The situation is hopeless."

As you can see, every situation for Jamie is an opportunity to reaffirm her underlying belief that she is an average fake. She has trouble internalizing anything positive about herself or owning the success she creates. Her belief system is like a pair of glasses through which she sees all of her experiences. Good or bad, her experiences serve as further proof of her negative self-image. What changes is only the degree of distortion required to fit them into her picture. In those worst-case scenarios (when dealing with the best of experiences) when no amount of distortion could succeed at re-shaping the event into the "evidence" she craves, Jamie simply discards the experience altogether, putting it aside as if it had never happened at all.

The words on these internal tapes vary from person to person depending on the beliefs that are being supported. The relentless, unforgiving and destructive nature of the self-talk, however, is consistent.

There are certain basic beliefs we have about ourselves, some of which we are not even aware of. These beliefs are the foundation for the tapes that play in our heads. If asked, we would probably deny a majority of these beliefs, but it is precisely these silent ones that we must become aware of. The more unconscious the belief, the more dangerous and powerful in shaping our interpretation of experiences. Our negative self-talk seeks out every opportunity to fit our present experience into our pre-existing self-image. It sees everything through the glasses that are our old beliefs. The two systems work together, each strengthening the other. Together, they are indeed a viable opponent. As always, however, their enemy is awareness.

Jamie and I explore her beliefs.

J: I just can't play after they show up; I'm a complete basket case.

N: Why is it difficult for you to keep playing well once you notice that your coach's next lesson has arrived?

J: I'm edgy because I know that my coach just wants to finish with me and get on to this other player. It's only because my coach is a professional and I'm paying him that he gives me the rest of my time.

N: Why does he want to get to this other player?

J: Because she's probably legitimate.

N: And what are you, the athlete who won last weekend's tournament?

J: I just know that he knows I'm not really a happening player. I think I'm just wasting his time and it's embarrassing for both of us to be there pretending I'm something. He makes a good show of it because he's a professional and needs the business, but I'm sure this other student really matters.

N: Why don't you matter?

J: I'm just a joke. He knows I'm not a serious player.

And there it is, the real belief: she's "a joke, not a serious player." *She* doesn't matter.

WHERE DID YOU GO?

By repeating these negative messages in the moments when she faces challenge, Jamie is abandoning herself at precisely the time when she most needs her own support. Walking onto the court, the moment when she needs to believe in herself most intensely, the moment when she is asking that self to do something very difficult and frightening, *this* is when she decides to turn her back on herself. She disowns this self (her self) and then turns around and sends "it" onto center court, all alone with only a pocketful of insults to hang on to. And amazingly, throughout this process, she was completely unaware of how she was treating herself.

Not only do we abandon ourselves through negative self-talk, but we choose competition and performance (the most difficult of all situations) as the time to ridicule and criticize a self that is already feeling scared and insecure. In case you have forgotten, this abandoned self is *you*. As a result, we are out there with nothing but angry, critical and self-hating spectators, all of them in our own mind. How could we feel supported and confident?

LISTEN CLOSELY

Don't despair, there is hope. As is always the case, the process of healing begins with awareness. We must first learn to notice *the way* we talk to ourselves. Because our internal dialogue is so habitual and seemingly so much a part of us, it may feel unnatural to notice or *watch* it, and yet this watching is necessary in order to change it. You must start to examine your mind's output as you would any other external product. What are the words you use to put yourself down? What are you whispering in your ear when the music is turned up? Take note of it. Become aware of how you undermine your own confidence. Notice your mind and its workings as you would study a guest at a party you're giving. That's what our mind is, a guest who has come to the party that is our life. Remember though, our mind knows us well, it's been to every party we've ever thrown. Think of your mind as the kid who throws spit balls at you but who sits empty-handed and smiling each time you try to catch him. Our thoughts know how to get us when we're not looking, how to make us believe that the reality we're living is the only way it can be. It's not.

WATCH IT

The first and most critical step in changing these beliefs is learning to *notice* your negative self-talk. Start listening for the messages you tell yourself, the specifics of how you undermine your confidence. Become a witness to your own insults. Remember, they go by quickly, sometimes without your even noticing. *Notice them.* We must create a pause button that we can press as each criticism appears in our mind, a net in which to catch the negativity. You may still believe these criticisms (and you most certainly will at the beginning), but this is to be expected. Why would they lose their meaning just because you see them? It is fruitless to yell back at your inner voice. Just start listening to *how* you talk to yourself. Put out a radar for the self-doubting, ever-critical voice that you live with every day. If, after you've done something well, you think to yourself "at least I do *one* thing well," *notice* that. If your habit is to caution yourself *not* to get too "full of yourself," (since after all, it's not like this means you're worth something), *notice* that. Whatever your particular style of abuse, notice it. *Notice all of it.*

KNOCK KNOCK

As you start to pay attention to your negative self-talk, listen for *whose* voice it is in your head. *Who* does it sound like? Who does it remind you of? Is it your mother's, father's, grandmother's, an old coach's? Examine the original basis for this person's criticism of you. What was his or her reason for thinking this about you? What age were you when this person became convinced of this? What was it, specifically, that led him or her to believe these hopeless things about you? By following this exploration back to the source, you may discover that *your* negative self-talk, the destructive messages you now feed yourself without any help from others, never were much in the way of truth. There may be little evidence to support these beliefs. What does exist probably occurred as a self-fulfilling prophecy, after you absorbed the messages and their corresponding identity. These beliefs (which have withstood the test of time) may not have been about you at all. And yet, because of the validity of their source or sources (and the nature of this source's relationship to you) such beliefs were exempt from the usual requirements for truth or fairness. Your mother said it, and since mothers only speak the truth, it was true and you were that.

In examining the specific messages of your negative self-talk, you may become aware of how closely *your* internal dialogue applies to the self-image of this original source. Sadly, parents often use their children as a place to put their feelings about themselves and their own lives. Continuing to invest meaning in these misplaced messages is a way of carrying on the family torch, keeping the connection alive with our families. This means continuing to sacrifice your *own* life because of problems that were never yours to begin with.

As you begin to realize how much you have suffered (and how little your now-present internal dialogue was originally related to you), there may be feelings of both rage and sadness. This is progress. Much of our experience in life is often lost in the misplaced agendas of others. You are entitled to whatever emotions arise. *You* are entitled to your own life, which includes your own vision of yourself.

With awareness can come a tendency to want to look away from the truth. It is painful to accept that your parents, the people who are supposed to do what's best for you, could have used you as a dumping ground for their own self-doubt and inadequacy. Accepting this requires looking at your parents in a new way. It is both tragic and frightening to realize how much of *your* time may have been lost, how the real you has not been able to thrive because of these invasive and imposed beliefs. At this stage you may feel the urge to push the truth away in order to avoid mourning what could have been, had you been able to believe in yourself.

From the journal of a dancer:

> *I think often of how much I could have accomplished, especially considering that this much talent has been able to make its way through the self-doubt and loathing. The fact is, there is a spirit in me which has fought back ferociously against the voices seeking to block and ruin my enjoyment . This spirit keeps me both hopeful and despairing. I think of all that I have wasted in myself, all the energy used just to combat these negative demons. How tarnished every good experience has been as a result of these beliefs. It is amazing to think of what I could do if I weren't blocking my path at every step, traveling five miles for every one forward, all that energy fighting those internal demons who refuse to believe in me.*

CHANGING THE CHANNEL

Becoming an observer of your own mind can have a powerful effect. In noticing your own mind's *cruelty*, the brutal manner in which you treat your self, you may also become aware of how much *you* have and are continuing to suffer at the hands of your own mind. It is sometimes easier to conceive of this suffering self as separate from the self who does the punishing and maligning. The tragedy is that they are both *you*. As you become more aware of your mind's activity, you may actually begin to feel genuine sadness for yourself, as if you were watching a child or good friend suffer. You may have the urge to defend yourself against this destructive part of you. This is good. The pure act of attempting to be gentle and speak kindly to yourself while noticing the hurtful self-talk you generate, can, in fact, end up teaching you to feel differently about *you*. Caring for yourself in a new way can lay the path toward a new vision of yourself, and consequently, a new you. Gradually this self, this you, starts to feel like an entity *worthy* of the better treatment you are offering it. Like a child who receives affection after years of abuse, eventually you too will respond to this conscious kindness and may even feel you deserve it.

Most importantly, acknowledging your own suffering can create a solid place from which to notice your own destructive thoughts. Compassion provides a safe shore from which to look out at the shark-infested waters of your mind. Regardless of what you have received or not received in the way of caring thus far in your life, you can change everything right now with one decision—the decision to be your own caretaker. As such, there is only one job requirement to which you must rigorously adhere, one truth which you must wholeheartedly accept. In this moment, you are the person who is responsible for relating to and treating *yourself* with kindness and compassion.

THE SUPPORTING CAST

In creating a new set of beliefs about yourself, do *not* underestimate the importance of something as simple as putting yourself in the company of people who are good for you, people who make you feel worthy and capable. You can learn from just being around a vision of yourself that is positive. Become *aware* and careful about who you spend your time with. *Notice* how you feel about *you* when in the company of the various players in your life. You may have never asked yourself if those with whom you choose to surround yourself are actually good for you. *Ask yourself!* Take a good look at those around you. People who re-affirm your negative self-image are *toxic*. There is much to be gained from limiting your contact with these folks. Weed out the toxic players as much as possible. Surround yourself with the people who see your potential, who strengthen, encourage and believe in the successful you. Examine those in your life whose support you "just assume." *Which you* are they supporting? Which *you* are they *willing* to support? Is it a successful you? Or, on the other hand, is it the disappointed, un-actualized you that they support? By remaining *this* you, do you *give* them something—a sense of purpose, a role in your life, a relationship with you that doesn't threaten *their* place? Does this you make them feel needed? Notice the role that resisting success and remaining stagnant plays in the relationships in your life. Start examining which *you* is being "supported" by the various players that surround you. Run down the list. Do you want to continue being this you? Is it worth giving up the you *you* want to be so that they can have the you *they* want? Do not take the importance of your relationships for granted. Put yourself in the company of those who support the you of your full potential.

Pam, a concert pianist, showed up at my office with the goal of, as she put it, "working out my relationship with my mother, and more to the point, the disastrous part my mother has played in my musical career." Over the months that we've been working together, both Pam and I have learned more about the problem. Together, we discovered and decided that Pam was better off *not* spending time with her mother just before performance. Still, despite her understanding, she sometimes fails to honor her own awareness, wishing for a different truth.

Recently she scheduled a visit with her mother on the Thursday before a weekend recital, convinced that her record of recent success would protect her from the worthless feelings her mother traditionally inspired. The visit was pleasant and everything was right on track for the performance. She was not concerned. Enthusiastically, Pam announced that she had recovered, her mother no longer held the power to destroy her confidence and power. She didn't give the visit with her mother another thought. As she put it, "I'm fine. The past is finally over."

Not surprisingly, the recital brought disaster. Pam felt insecure and made mistakes she had not made in years. She was completely unable to get comfortable or trust her own skill. Worst of all, the self-hatred and humiliation that followed the performance was of a previous and dangerous era, one when she could not recover *any* sense of self-worth after a fall from perfection. Pam was baffled and horrified, particularly because nothing negative had transpired between her and her mother during their visit. Even worse than the actual errors she made was the fury of self-loathing that followed, a fury she had not felt in a long time. Each error was magnified to epic proportion; she felt humiliated and ashamed by her failure. Despite a long run of success, Pam was reduced to utter nothingness. Her mistakes were cause for the total annihilation of everything she had ever accomplished or ever was, performer or human being. Later, she confessed the extent of her self-punishment. "The suffering was so intense that I considered giving up the piano entirely. It just wasn't and isn't worth this much torment. The fact that I was imperfect, or that I distrusted my own insight and went ahead and scheduled a visit with my mother right before an important performance, these I could probably live with. What is intolerable though, is how pathetic it is that I am still allowing my mother to do this to me. I am pathetic for still letting it happen." The fact that Pam was still vulnerable to her mother made all of her accomplishments feel meaningless. In her own eyes, Pam remained a helpless child, completely under the control of her omnipotent mother. Adulthood seemed impossible. Her mother could still take it all away in the blink of an eye, and consequently, her mother still owned her success. Nothing belonged to Pam, not even her feelings about herself. Everything was available to destruction by this mother.

Temporarily, Pam believed that until she was safe from her mother's influence, until that day when being with her mother had no affect on her performance, she would remain a non-entity, completely invisible and powerless. Only one of them could hold the power and clearly it was her mother. How much could her success mean, how real was it if it could be taken away so easily? She could not trust her own confidence and was always in danger of losing its grasp. Her achievements felt worthless.

These beliefs, along with her paralyzing self-hatred, eventually faded and she returned to the confident and successful musician she was. And yet, no matter how successful, Pam finally understood that she had no choice but to remain forever cognizant of her mother's affect on her. Once her mother was in the picture, not only did her hard work and confidence cease to exist, but her very enthusiasm and connection to her passion dried up as well. Like an injection of poison, Pam's mother took up residence inside her, maintaining an internal presence long after she had physically left the scene. It was this presence then that turned Pam into the laughing stock of her own internal audience, re-inspiring the hateful and mocking audience she had worked so hard to quiet. Maybe some day she would be able to change this reaction, but for now she decided simply to avoid her mother before performances. The helplessness she felt about having to do this paled in comparison to that which her mother's presence created in her. Pam was making the decision to work *with* what was rather than trying to deny it because it was painful, to stop punishing herself and failing on the stage in an effort to make what was into what should be.

In accepting her past and the affect it had on her, it was important for Pam to understand that she did *not* have to become immune to her mother in order for her success to mean something. The voice telling her that she would continue to be nothing until she had fully killed off her mother, was in fact, a part of the very voice she was trying to destroy. The day may come when her mother does not destroy her belief in herself, and then again it may not. Regardless, this is about Pam's relationship with her mother and not her talent. The focus must go to what *you* know about yourself, what *you* have accomplished separate from your parents or your past. Who are you as a performer? Who is the you that you have created? No matter what you suffer at the hands of your past, you will indeed return to this present you. Accept, however, that it may take a little time. The fact that your past can affect you only means that you are human. The performer you have become remains unchanged.

I asked Pam to write me a letter in which she described how she would handle the situation with her mother differently in the future. She writes: "I have come to regard my relationship with my mother as I do snakes in the desert while hiking. I must continue to climb the mountain but remain ever-conscious of protecting myself from danger. I will be extra careful to preserve my strength when approaching a difficult pass. When I do get bitten (which is inevitable) I will treat myself with compassion and remember that what I am experiencing is simply the nature of life. I will refrain from judging myself for being susceptible to the animal's poison, since judgment only intensifies the symptoms and makes the recovery-time longer. Most of all, I will accept that whether I like it or not, the venom will have to run its course through my system before I can return to climbing. No matter how bad it gets or how much I doubt my own survival, I must trust that, in time, I will indeed return to my normal state of strength and resume my position on the mountain."

NEW VOICES

Keep in mind, negative self-talk takes a very long time to disappear; sometimes it never goes away, but it does change. Do *not* be discouraged or feel that you are not "there" yet because your negative self-talk continues to play. It may always play. But *you* can do something different with it. When you catch yourself self-abusing, *turn* the tables. Use it as an opportunity to say something *kind* to yourself, to recognize what you have been able to accomplish in the face of such discouragement. Think of comforting yourself in relation to what is happening inside you. The more loving you can be toward yourself, the more you will *teach* that self how *you* in fact deserve to be treated.

7

OVERCOMING NEGATIVITY

~

*T*hroughout this book I have written a good deal about negativity and the role it plays in the performer's life. It comes up in a myriad of ways: self-talk, self-doubt, self-loathing, self-criticism, insecurity, envy, unhappiness, fear. The list is endless. It is there and it must be dealt with. But how? How do we keep our negativity from overwhelming us and burying or snuffing out our potential. How do we wrestle back our talent from the jaws of a force that seems to hate us?

Performance literature offers us two major suggestions for dealing with negativity. The first approach is to look at our negative thoughts as bad habits. Our negativity is seen as an activity that we have learned, and therefore something that we can unlearn. In this case, negativity is seen as something more physiological than psychological, a sort of faulty wiring system in the brain that must be interrupted. The body needs to be re-programmed to feel and act positively. Negative thoughts are seen as pits in the mind that we fall into. By replacing a negative thought with a positive one, we are literally filling in that pit, retraining the bad habit to be a good one, replacing the cigarette with a walk in the park, if you will.

There is a belief too, that repeating positive things to ourselves (enough of them anyway) creates a trickle-down effect. By telling ourselves good things, re-parenting ourselves in a sense, we can literally learn to believe that these good things about us are true. By repeating the positive, we are training ourselves not only to behave in a different way but to feel differently about ourselves as well.

For this group of believers, peak performance is a physical and mental state that can be manufactured. There is a way of training to be in this peak state, a way that the body can remember this state and re-create it when it counts. As performers therefore, we must learn how to create and maintain our personal peak states so that our bodies will have the conditions they need in order to shine.

While this very action-oriented approach is still quite prevalent in the performance literature, the last decade has brought a slight addition to the way the field is dealing with negativity in performance. The addition, simply put, has to do with the way we are supposed to talk to our negative feelings. While the old system instructed us to replace our negative thoughts with positive ones because there was no place for negativity in the performer's life, the newer model makes an effort to at least admit that the negativity exists. In this system we are taught to acknowledge the fear, doubt, insecurity or whatever it is that has shown up. Let's say you were a singer preparing to walk out on stage and are experiencing fright and a sense of fragility. The old model might have counseled you to ignore these feelings while saying to yourself: "I'm psyched, I can't wait to go and sing." The updated script on the other hand, would start a bit differently, as in: "I acknowledge that I'm afraid but I still want to go out and sing."

While their approaches are a bit different, these methods maintain similar philosophies. Both treat negativity as something that is not to be dealt with, a part of life that has to be gotten around or ignored in order to succeed. In the first, what I call the "bad habit" system, this is more obvious. When setting up your peak state you don't let in your negative feelings at all. You shun them, do away with them, and insist that they are different than how they actually feel. In the "acknowledge" system, while the feelings are spoken about, they remain "wrapped up," shiny and packaged, as if all the negativity could be scooped up from inside us and contained in a big vat—unexplored—something you recognize from the outside but not something you are going to feel, understand or deal with.

Put simply, these systems do not work. The reasons are multiple. To begin with, negative thoughts are far more than bad habits, far more than just thoughts. Behind those thoughts are deep-seated beliefs about ourselves. It is the belief behind the thoughts or words that gives them such weight and staying power. Most of us have been suffering with the same negative thoughts about ourselves for our entire lives. If you imagine the negative words to be a dingy bobbing in the sea, that dingy is tied to a heavy anchor, otherwise known as our internal belief system. This is the real thing we're contending with here. The fact that our negative thoughts are actually beliefs means that they have histories; there are strong associations and experiences tied into them. They are more than just thoughts; they are whole senses we have about ourselves, ways we relate to ourselves, ways we determine our very identities. They are part of the fabric of our being. Negative self-perceptions are big and old, far bigger and far older than anything that "substituting a positive" can affect on any deep level.

In line with this, to consider a negative thought to be a bad habit is once again to underestimate the thought's meaning. Bad habits are something that you can replace or quit cold turkey. Negative thoughts come from negative beliefs, and these are not something we can just quit. They are part of who we are.

With regard specifically to the "acknowledge" approach to performance negativity, I have found that most people do not know what it actually means to acknowledge their feelings. The process of acknowledging begins and ends with simply saying the words, and thus doesn't translate into any kind of feeling change or growth. As one tennis player expressed, "So great I acknowledge it. Now I know it; it knows it; we all know it and damn it, it's still there, and I still have to go and play. Remind me how my problem has changed?"

Undoubtedly, it does save a lot of energy to not have to pretend we're not afraid. The problem is that we are still afraid, and we are not (in this approach) taught what then to do with this fear or how to help ease it. The idea behind this philosophy is that the feeling will ease simply by being acknowledged, not felt, not experienced, just acknowledged. In my professional and personal experience, however, I have discovered that in order for the feelings to really change, far more is needed in this process than just the words of acknowledgment.

While different in some ways, both of the approaches I have examined thus far share the same fundamental flaw. The way we as performers have been taught to deal with negativity is to avoid feeling it, push it aside, make it go away. After all, why would one want to feel something that is bad? This is a large question and one that I will address later. I will say, however, that it is not just performers in our society that are told to stay away from bad feelings. It is a cultural code of sorts. Bad feelings are bad and must be avoided at all cost. Avoiding or ignoring them is our only defense against them.

As a society there are a number of beliefs we hold, whether spoken or not, about negative feelings. The first is that our negative feelings will overwhelm us if we attempt to feel them in any way. If we go near them, they will take over our lives like a river that just washes over our being, sweeps us up in its horror. If we let in or admit to our negative feelings, we will certainly behave negatively. Our negative feelings are awarded an enormous amount of power. Certainly there will be no way to "hear from" a negative feeling without acting it out. If we "make room" for the idea that we're sad, surely we will hurl ourselves in front of a train. Feeling a negative feeling in this culture is synonymous with behaving negatively and living a negative life. So too, we see negative feelings as *not* healable. They are there, stuck, forever the same. They cannot change. The only way we imagine their changing is with enough positive things happening in our lives. If enough spectacular things happen, then maybe they might change, but certainly not by anything that could happen on the inside. As if this were not enough, performers have an extra burden to carry when it comes to negative feelings. There is a belief that really gifted performers are not supposed to have any negative feelings. It is as if negative feelings make them not "real" performers, not stars. As a performer (one who is going to make it) you are supposed to be born free of negativity, completely believing in yourself, with no doubt and no fear. Nary a negative thought may have passed through your purely positive and sparklingly clean mind or you are forever tarnished. Performers are thus known to hide their true feelings, to cover up their scarlet letter, which in this case is that they are human!

Rest assured, performers are humans. Humans have positive and negative feelings. Performers have positive and negative feelings. Every single one of them. I have worked with and known hundreds, even thousands, of performers. Not one of them, no matter the level, is free of negative feelings. There is no more to say; it is a universal condition.

Given the way we view negative feelings, that they will overwhelm, control, and destroy us, that they are un-healable, that we will never get out of them, and that we are not supposed to have them, it is no wonder that we create the system we do. In our minds, we set up a nice, clean room where there exists only positive thoughts. We go inside that room and lock the door super tight. We add some double bolts, a chain and maybe a chair to sit up against it. On the other side of this door sits all the negative feelings we harbor, all the doubt, guilt, shame, insecurity, upset, worry and whatever else life has brought us. Our heads tell us we have successfully shut out all the difficult stuff while our bodies know otherwise. Our bodies, after all, are still carrying this other stuff. Our heads tell us we can ignore our bodies, that we can escape them if we just stay inside our "happy" room. This system does not work. It is a plan that limits not only our ability to perform but also our ability to live.

The reasons why this "locked door" system doesn't work are manifold. I will name only a few. To begin with, trying to keep these negative feelings out demands a tremendous amount of energy. We go through a lot of internal machinations just trying to make sure we don't hear from some of our actual feelings or beliefs. We end up, whether consciously or unconsciously, living in fear of these darker places inside us. While we hope that our locks stay tight, we can never know the force of our negativity, when it might break the door down and us with it. As a result, we cannot ever get truly comfortable; we are not really in control. There is, after all, this dark storm awaiting us on the other side of our imaginary door. Even when this fear is not conscious, it is still there because the body always knows what it is holding, whether it is allowed to address it or not.

It is precisely because these negative beliefs are shunned that they gain so much power. We have come to think that we cannot let them in, that such a thing would kill us. Hence, the importance of monitoring them becomes tantamount to survival. We unknowingly and unfortunately award them their very power by determining them as inadmissible. Anyone *not* allowed at the party will desperately want to be there and eventually end up crashing it!

Overcoming Negativity

Performing with these cast out negative beliefs is a difficult venture. For one thing, we are disconnected from aspects of ourselves and are thus operating from a disconnected center. Often I work with performers who talk about not being able to feel their feet on stage or who have the feeling of losing connection with themselves while performing.

Kevin, a musician, came to see me with precisely this sort of problem. This 29-year-old saxophonist was very upset about a recent concert he had given. In it, he had lost "connection" with himself and had the feeling of "not being able to play from his strength." As he explained, he needed to be in touch with his "essence" while he was playing. Although he had played the right notes and it was certainly an OK gig, he knew the performance lacked passion and the kind of fire that great jazz requires. He confessed too, that it had not been a fun experience because he couldn't "get in" to himself. He simply wasn't there.

This is where we began. I asked him a lot of questions about that night's performance and discovered that a series of disasters had occurred leading up to his going on stage. To start with, his trip to the gig had been fraught with traveler's nightmares. Secondly, instead of performing first, the diva of the evening had decided she wanted to go on before him and so he had gotten bumped from opening act to closing act, which meant a difference of four hours. In addition to all of this, his promoter had had a "melt down" which included attacking Kevin for things unrelated to his performance. Lastly, in the audience had sat Kevin's whole family and two of his old music teachers. A stressful situation? Not according to Kevin. When I mentioned that it sounded like a stressful gig to me, he was quick to explain that while there were a lot of things to deal with, letting it affect him was a different thing entirely and this is what being a pro was all about. "When you're a pro, you're tough, you don't let this kind of crap get in the way of your tunes."

As I learned more about him, I got to know the part of him that strongly believed that being a pro meant *not* getting nervous and not allowing anything to bother him. There were two very distinct and conflicting parts of Kevin. The first was the one that was living all this stressful stuff, feeling overwhelmed, terrified, pressured, irritated, frustrated and like he wanted to bolt. And the other was the one that believed that pros didn't get nervous, didn't let anything distract them from their music and were always ready to go out there and play, no matter what. This second part had a whole story, a family, memories, a certain logic, a set of people it wanted to be like and, as I came to find out, one person in particular it desperately did not want to be like. This "tough pro" part in Kevin had lots of reasons why it was not OK to "make room for" or "welcome" the nervous feelings inside him, lots of reasons why the stressed-out part of him was not allowed to be acknowledged. As far as this "tough pro" place was concerned, offering the "anxious place" a seat at the table would have been tantamount to failure.

Consequently, Kevin walked onto the floor that night with a body that was stressed, overwhelmed, afraid, and irritated and a head that was reminding him what being a pro required while simultaneously criticizing and being disappointed in him for having the experience that he was actually having! He picked up his sax, screaming at his nervous part to shut up, telling it that he would never be anybody if he couldn't deal with stress, that he had to be tough so that the audience and his band would know he was one of the "big guys." That night he played with a body whose experience was not welcome, had been dis-invited. He then wondered why that unwelcome body wasn't able to participate more fully on stage.

This is precisely what happens when we send the message to our bodies that only a part of what it is carrying is welcome. We become ungrounded, without a sense of wholeness, literally split off from ourselves. We cannot count on ourselves in such a state as there is no us to count on. It feels as if anything could happen, and indeed sometimes the unthinkable does happen when those negative beliefs bust through and make themselves known. But even when self-sabotage does not ensue, such a disconnected exper-ience on stage is terrifying and disruptive to a satisfying performance.

To ask ourselves to perform in a state of split-off-ness is to abandon ourselves at precisely the moment when we need ourselves the most. In the moments of performance, those moments that demand everything, we need most of all to be whole, connected, grounded and solid. This means that all of our parts must be welcome on stage. When the difficult or suffering parts are not welcome, there is an overall sense that we are not OK as we are, not a somebody that we can really support and believe in. This is hardly a message that will enhance or bring comfort to ourselves during those precious and ever-so-demanding moments that make up a per-formance. How can we expect to trust ourselves when we don't trust ourselves? How can we ever expect these negative places to heal when we continually abandon them and deem them unwelcome?

There is another reason why this "lock out" system doesn't work, one that is larger than anything I have discussed thus far. Fundamentally, such a system of denial or split-off-ness prevents our negative beliefs from healing. It leaves them frozen. What is split off or unfelt remains stagnant; it cannot change. As I see it, our goal is not just to get by without having these negative beliefs break through and destroy us. No, the goal is bigger. We are wanting to heal these beliefs, to make them change so that we can feel different. What does it mean to fully feel a feeling, to actually experience it in a way that allows it to shift? This brings me to the next discussion, namely, what creates change.

Change begins with how we envision our internal selves. If we see ourselves as existing in a uni-state, feeling one thing at one time, made up of one emotion, then it is no wonder we need to screen out anything negative. We need to choose the positive state considering it is our total experience. The self, however, is not like this. Not to turn us all into multiple personality types, but the fact is that the self contains many different parts, which can feel completely contradictory emotions at the same time. One part of us may feel we can do anything in the world we set our minds to and another part may feel (with just as much sureness) that we are incapable of becoming a true success. One part may know that our families support us wholeheartedly in our success while a neighboring part may believe that to succeed would mean to abandon and betray our families altogether.

Overcoming Negativity

In the end, everything resolves itself in contradiction. We have multiple parts with multiple beliefs. There is no *one* inner truth, no *one* state of being. Wholeness and health come about when we can make a "place" for all of our parts, when we can open up a dialogue between all of the parts of ourselves so that they are in relationship with, rather than at odds with one another. It is about changing our internal experience from a "but" universe to an "and" universe. That is to say, from an internal universe where one belief cancels out another that is contradictory to a state in which two contradictory beliefs can sit side by side with equal space being made for each. When there is room for all the parts of ourselves, we need not live in fear of those parts whose message we don't like. Those parts can be there as just that, parts of us, but not the whole of us and certainly not who we fundamentally "are." The process of wholeness and healing begins with making a "space" for all of our parts.

But what does it mean to make a space for these parts that hold negative beliefs? To begin with, it means accepting that all of the negative feelings we have are attached to larger stories. If we are aware of a sense of dread as we walk out on stage, we can be sure that that dread has a whole story to it, a history, memories, relationships, experiences, and most importantly, beliefs about us and our potential. That sense of dread does not begin and end on the stage. Rather, it is just a tiny spark emanating from a much larger "place" inside us. What if we were to view this spark of dread as an invitation to go inside, to find out what the whole of this dread is about, to discover why this place feels so in danger at the prospect of exposing itself? Or perhaps, it is not about exposing itself that this place feels dread. Perhaps it is about shining brightly, or falling short, or surpassing dad, or being right, or being wrong, or changing existing relationships, or any other of an infinite number of things.

The point is, only this place inside us can tell us what is making it feel dread. The idea is to approach this part of ourselves with a sense of curiosity and openness, to ask it what it knows, what it believes. Instead of running from an internal part that seems scary, what if we were to turn toward it and let it know that we were going to listen to it, acknowledge it, hear how it actually feels, how it has been for it, what it is afraid of and what it might need to feel differently.

I realize that it is a radical shift to consider this approach. This kind of process demands that we be truly open and curious as to what this "negative" part has to say. No matter how much havoc it has wreaked in our lives, we cannot approach it with an attitude that it needs to change. Rather, we must be accepting and interested in hearing it exactly as it is, not asking it to change, not telling it why it is wrong, not giving it the reasons why its argument makes no sense and doesn't fit with reality. It does fit with its reality! Furthermore, we cannot demand that this negative feeling change. We cannot expect it to be anything other than what it actually is, no matter how un-real the other parts of us consider its beliefs. *How* we approach these negative places inside ourselves is the most important part of the process. Can we really be open to hearing from parts of ourselves that seem to hate us, doubt us, want to do away with us? It is important for us to get comfortable asking questions of these parts. It is sometimes helpful to ask not only what these parts think of us, but what the intention of holding onto this belief is. Or, what purpose this belief served when it first began. At some point there may have been a protective quality to our negative beliefs. Recently I worked with a singer who was struggling with a feeling that she couldn't sing or as she put it, "part of her wouldn't let her sing." This part of her told her that she was too inept to even imagine that she could do something as special as singing. Understandably, she hated this part and viewed it as her enemy. Given that hating it wasn't making it any less fierce of an opponent, we decided to turn towards this place in her and approach it with openness and interest, asking what it felt, what the core feeling at the center of it was.

What we discovered was that its primary emotion, the feeling that motivated its insults, was in fact fear. As we probed further in trying to understand what made it so afraid, we learned that it was afraid to show any kind of joy. Knowing this woman's history, I also knew that in her family, showing any kind of feeling, particularly being excited about anything resulted in severe humiliation. She was made fun of for having emotions. Singing for her was all about showing her emotions, being joyful, getting OK with her passion.

Putting her choking part into this broader context, we began to understand its fear more deeply. We could now see how it had originally intended to protect her, to see to it that she was spared any further suffering or humiliation. Believe it or not, this part did have her best interest at heart and wasn't aware that its protection was no longer necessary. Had we listened only to its insults, judged it merely by the weapons it used to defend itself, we would have never known its truth, never known that it was on her side. In essence, we would have left it alone to suffer in silence, pausing long enough only to feel its affects, rather than know its experience. What is important in the curiosity of these negative parts is that we enter the *part's* experience, find out what it feels and why it came to feel the way it does—to offer it the benefit of the doubt even when it seems like it might be dangerous to do so. Knowing the choking place's intention allowed this singer to change her relationship with this part of herself from one of hatred and fear to one of compassion, understanding and even gratitude. With these new feelings coming toward it, the choke in her throat actually faded away and she was able to use her voice in a more joyful way.

These various parts of ourselves have their own wisdom and logic. They know things to which our intellectual minds are not privy. Sometimes it is not because our feelings toward the negative part have shifted that the negative part heals (as was the case with our singer). But rather, it heals because the negative part itself lets us know what it needs in order to change. Fascinatingly enough, the negative part's solution is often phrased in words our "heads" could never have formulated or imagined.

The following is from part of a session with Alice, an equestrian.

> A: I am so pissed off. I was riding great and then I realized that K, my trainer, knew how well I was riding. He got really excited and started talking about all these plans we were going to make with new horses and that kind of thing. I could just tell he knew we were a good team and that I was pretty damn good. At that moment I got this unbelievable sense of doom, like 'oh no, now I'll never be able to come through, now I am sure to blow it.'

N: How did you treat this place of doom you en-countered?

A: I got really angry with it. I think I just tried to suppress it and tell it that it was being silly, that I really was a great rider and to basically shut up.

N: So what happened?

A: I totally blew it and my trainer was really disappointed, of course. He didn't say anything, but I could just tell. I felt like, once again, I couldn't rally to the challenge. I had to go away with him being disappointed. And even worse, the mistake I made in the next round was a totally amateurish mistake. It was like I was just not able to let him think I was a real star. I couldn't let myself have it. I am so angry with this part of me because it always wins; it always blows it for me. It's not like I didn't recognize it, I did. I told it to go away, but it still got me.

N: So what if we were to explore what this place that "got you" is all about. What is it that this place can't tolerate? Is it something to do with your success, a feeling with your trainer, this particular situation or what?

A: (After paying attention inside for a few minutes) It seems to have something to do with his expectations of me or his belief about me.

N: So something about your trainer's belief or expectation of you is intolerable?

A: Not exactly. It's like I or this place can't tolerate his thinking that we are this great team.

N: Ah...so it's something about the team?

A: More like...something about his being excited about me.

N: So this place doesn't believe or isn't comfortable with his being excited about you?

A: Right, that's it.

N: Can you check there if the word uncomfortable fits exactly right?

A: It's more like this place can't sit with that idea of his. It makes it anxious, his believing that I'm that. Yeah, like I had to go and kill off his excitement.

N: Can you sense inside what gets it so anxious about his being excited about you? Is it anxious that he might think you were a good rider, a success or perhaps something else?

A: It's anxious about his believing I'm a pro, that I don't get nervous, and that I know my job and all of that. That's why I had to go make this completely beginner mistake. This part insists on letting him know that he can't count on me. He has to be shown that I am not a reliable contender, that I always have these mistakes in me waiting to happen.

(She talks more about this.)

I don't know how to work with this place. I know what it wants to do to me, but I can't stop it.

N: What does this place believe about you? Can you ask it?

A: (tears) It believes that I will and can never come through consistently, that I can't be the one that K believes in, that I am not the one to bet on. I know what it believes and still it never changes. At the very least, I would like to know how to keep it from interrupting my performance. I mean it can keep believing whatever it wants, I just need to come up with a retort to it that will protect me from sabotaging myself.

N: So maybe we might want to ask it what it would need to hear so as to quiet it in these moments.

A: (After a five-minute pause and then a smile) It needs me to own my own place, not to worry about K or anyone else. When I think about being this good rider, really being that, taking it on, putting my focus there in my own body…then it seems to ease.

N: What specifically might it need to hear in these moments to leave you alone?

A: (laughing) Be in your own body Alice, it tells me. Let it begin and end with me. Yes, that helps. It's odd but saying that it is just between me and me and no one else really means something to this place. It's like no one else needs to know that I'm a pro for it to be true. Only me. I think it needs me to turn my attention to me and away from all these other forces. Within this kind of dialogue I land within myself, and the whole proving thing gets detoxified. I can get on with my own work.

I had been working with Alice for a period of months at the time of this dialogue, and she had become quite comfortable foraging around in her internal territory. As a result, the process of going and seeing what her "places" had to say was somewhat unencumbered, the dialogue between the part of her that was listening and that which was telling its story had become almost natural. Furthermore, Alice and I had been working for quite some time with this particular "reliable pro place." However, it wasn't until this particular session that it provided her with the path to its own resolution, generously letting her in on the very thing it needed to feel differently. She never could have come up with or guessed its response had she not been willing to go inside and hear from the part itself. By spending time with the "negative" belief, the one answer that mattered became clear.

In another example, an internal shift and experience of relief came when a client was able to discover the precise feeling that was at the core of a whole negative sense inside her. Lena was a violinist who came in with "a big problem." Each time Lena played in front of a group of musicians she would become "nervously stuck," "unable to make anything happen with her instrument." And yet, oddly, she was fine in front of an audience of non-musicians.

She explained that her nervousness had something to do with proving that she was "one of them" and good enough to

Overcoming Negativity

play in the company of "real" musicians. She felt certain that she wasn't good enough to be judged by those who knew the truth about music. As I watched her explain this, it appeared to me that although what she was saying was feasible and perhaps true as well, she was not really asking the nervously stuck place itself what it was nervous about, what it believed about her as a violinist (and a person), and thus why it felt stuck in front of other musicians. Here are excerpts from our dialogue:

> *N: Where, I wonder, do you experience this crippling nervousness in your body when it comes on?*
>
> *L: It's sort of a tightness in my chest.*
>
> *N: So it's this feeling of not being able to prove yourself that sits in your chest?*
>
> *L: I think so.*
>
> *N: Can you sit for a moment with this, not being able to prove yourself. See if there is a little give in your chest or just notice what happens as you take this in...that you're not going to be able to prove yourself with those who know better.*
>
> *L: (After some time) No, I don't get anything. But something else comes as I pay attention to that part of my chest. It's as if I'm in a bind. It feels trapped. Yes, it has to do two different things that are at odds with each other.*
>
> *(Time passes)*
>
> *L: Yes, it has to do with not being humiliated but not being too good.*
>
> *(Time passes)*

L: (She breaks out with a sigh) That's it, it's trapped! It has to prove to these musicians that it is good enough, but it can't make them think that I think I'm somebody important. So it's this delicate balance that I can't always find. That's exactly it. I have to land somewhere in the middle. They have to think I'm good, but then they can't think that I think I'm good.

Lena had experienced the first step of change. She had found what this place in her was struggling with, its handle if you will. This place was trapped between the two tasks it needed to fulfill. The kind of shift she experienced in this session almost always brings a sense of physical relief (like an internal sigh) as the body becomes aware of what it has really been living. In the weeks that followed, this "trapped" place in her continued to open and tell its story. Eventually, knowing the story it carried, which again, could never have been guessed or formulated by her "head," brought relief and a resolution to the problem. She felt differently performing in front of other musicians once she knew what her body had been carrying regarding this issue.

The system I am proposing is one in which we view every negative thought or feeling as coming from a bigger place or part inside us. The bigger place has a story, a whole experience of its own. It knows certain things, feels certain things, suffers with certain difficulties. Envision these internal places, if you can, as entities in their own right. With this approach, every negative feeling we have is an invitation in, an opportunity to get better acquainted with one of our places. Imagine a negative feeling as a flag being held up, alerting us that an internal area needs attending to.

Overcoming Negativity

It is up to us to determine how we attend to these negative-carrying places inside us. Often they are places of great suffering. The most important thing is to bring an attention to them that is open, curious and welcoming. We must listen to the perspective of the negative place itself; hear what it has to say in its own words. This kind of listening requires that we de-center from our "head" or the part of us that is determined to make the negative disappear. One thing I know for sure, the negative won't leave us alone until we let it say its peace.

So how does this work, this making space for our internal places, welcoming them and hearing how it is from their perspective? Imagine again the internal room we create, where the negative is not let in but shut out on the other side of the door. These negative parts of us are real entities filled with lived experience. As long as these parts know that they are not welcome, they will yell, scream, bang and try to break down the door. Wouldn't you if you knew you were not allowed into the space where everyone else is living? They are being shut out of your life. The remarkable thing is that the instant you unlock the door and let them know that they are welcome, that you will listen to them, they immediately ease. Knowing that they are going to be included, they relax; their urgency and intensity instantly lessens. There is no longer a need to sabotage you in order to make their presence known. By deciding to listen, you are offering them another way to be known, one that no longer requires that they act. While locked out of your inner space, their only option is to show up by ruining your performance. Once they can be heard from, they don't have to do this.

A case in point: Allison, a musician, struggled with a need to control everything that went on in her performance. The feeling got in her way and was interrupting her ability to relax into her playing. Gradually, we came to a better understanding of what was "in" her need to control and how she had needed to be in control when she was a child, that the intention of her controlling urge had, in fact, been to save her life. Allison was the child of a single parent who was severely depressed and paranoid. From a very young age she had been in charge of not only her own basic needs, but her mother's as well. The family's very survival depended upon Allison's resourcefulness. With this better understanding of what her controlling was really about, she devised a new system, one that came directly from the part of her that *did* the controlling. When we asked "it" what it needed from her so as not to have to act out on stage, the words that came were "to not be abandoned." It wanted her to recognize how it had saved her life, done what it had to do. It told us that no one had acknowledged the job it had performed, but instead had criticized it as rigid and manipulative and in the end, told it that it was unwelcome. If it had gone away, she would have never survived. This truth she came to honor. The image then that appeared for my client was one of a monkey that she would sit on her shoulder during her performances. Her monkey symbolized that part of her that felt it was necessary to control. It was welcome there and could just come along for the ride as a friend, rather than an enemy. The plan seemed to please the controlling place (now the monkey) as it never again felt the need to act out on stage.

While all of these examples represent just the first steps toward change, nonetheless, they are critically important. What then is it that allows for these changes to happen?

Overcoming Negativity

What causes a negative feeling to shift? In my experience as a performer as well as a therapist, there are two fundamental processes that can make this happen. The first, to which I have referred a number of times, is the process of attending to the negative place inside us from *its* side, hearing what it has to say without interrupting it, even when what it has to say is very difficult to hear. We have all had the experience of feeling bad or sad about something. When we go to a friend and talk about it, very often the friend (before even having heard the whole story) will tell us why it is silly to have our bad feeling, how it makes no sense, is not true, etc. etc. After telling us why our feeling is uncalled-for, he or she will usually tell us all the things we need to be doing to make the feeling go away. Despite their good intentions, our bad feeling is no more tolerable in their internal system than their own bad feelings. It must, therefore, be annihilated. This task that others take on in our culture is mistakenly labeled friendship. When I leave conversations like this (usually quickly), I feel worse, not better. I now not only have the original bad feeling (which is entirely intact and un-changed), but on top of it, I feel bad about having the bad feeling. And, I'm anxious because I have a whole list of things I know I immediately have to do to fix it. While the original bad feeling now has lots of new bad feelings to keep it company, it itself feels uncomforted, unheard, and unknown, as do I.

Regardless of whether our bad feelings make sense to our heads, they still make sense to this "gut" place within us. It doesn't matter how much logic we hurl at these places, it still feels bad inside. A different thing happens when we sit with a friend who is able to really listen to us. Unlike the first friend, this person may say very little, but we have the sense that they "get" what the bad feeling is, what it is really about, that they can let it exist. While we may not explore the whole story, the part of us carrying it feels heard. It has been attended to, someone has made space for it, not demanded its resolution. This is the most important experience we can have. It is a process that, amazingly, we can also provide for ourselves. This is what it means to make space for our own difficult feelings, attending to them in this manner, letting them know that their perspective and their experience is welcome and will be listened to. This makes all the difference in the world. It is as if we are deciding to sit down next to our difficult feelings and let them know that they can finally relax, that rather than screaming at them to go away, telling them that there is no ear for them, no shoulder, at last they can have the experience of being sat with, of being comforted and heard. In the very same way that we feel differently after a friend listens to us in this manner, the difficult feelings do as well.

There is another important element in creating change that I call *formulating the unformulated*. So much of what we feel, sense or experience remains in a sort of unformulated state, like embryonic fluid swirling around in us. The process of getting to know what a part of us really feels and believes is like scooping up all that fluid and making it into an actual entity. The sense we have been carrying about somebody or a situation or ourselves, can become a "something" that we can relate to. The act of scooping up or finding the story means gathering up what we have been living with in a vague way and making it clear, defined. The act of making the vague sense into a clear "something" immediately creates change. Once there is a set of beliefs or feelings to relate to, then we are not *it*. There is an I and an *it*. The negative feelings become an *it* that we are in relation to, a part whose history and experience we can begin to know. But we are not *it*. This is a critical shift. At the moment when it becomes a "something," and "not us," the negative part instantly loses the bulk of its power. Its beliefs become less of an unconscious "given." We can work with a negative "something" within us but a negative us is a daunting enemy.

At the same time that we are vastly reducing the power of these negative parts, so too, we are shifting our point of view or the point of identity that we are looking at the problem from. Instead of being in the midst of some vague noxious gas that we are not separate from, formulating the story that has been as yet unformulated, bringing the vague sense into focus, actually creates a safe shore from which we can get to know and deconstruct this negative stuff. When we can see the negative place as a "something" and not us, we are suddenly identified with the us who has been living with and feeling this negative part. There is a sense of compassion that develops for ourselves in having to endure this negativity. It is as if we shift from being aligned with the negative part to being aligned with, or part of, the us that is being battered by it. Once compassion is there for ourselves, we can start asking this negative "something" questions about why it does and says these awful things to us, why it wants to harm us and so on. It is at this point that we can gain some control and get rooted in the "good" us who is being mistreated.

The shifting of our point of view is particularly important with feelings that don't want to change. I have talked thus far about the process that allows negative parts of ourselves to change and believe new things. I would be fibbing however, if I said that every negative place will in fact shift and evolve into something more positive through the process of attending to and *formulating the unformulated*.

Some negative places remain equally intact no matter how much we openly listen to them, understand them, know their origins, and are aligned with ourselves in having to live with them. There they are, showing up at the party with the very same nasty things to say to us. These unchanging negative parts may never give up their terrible beliefs about us, but how we interact with them can change. Sometimes it is helpful to let this negative part of yourself know that you hear what it has to say, but that nonetheless, it is not the only opinion that matters and it may not be able to get what it wants.

A friend recently described a scenario in her family when one of her three children desperately did not want to go away on vacation. My friend and her husband did everything they could to convince the five-year-old that she would have fun on the trip. In the end, the little girl still did not want to go. And so the family let her know that her "no" had been duly noted, but that she would still have to go on vacation. Further, she would not be expected to change from the "no" camp to the "yes" camp once there; she could simply be there as the representative of the "no's." This, the little girl liked. Dealing with a negative place that refuses to change its opinion can be a bit like dealing with a child who refuses to go on vacation. At some point you can let this negative place know that you hear how it feels, but that its feelings are not going to be heeded, that you have a different opinion of yourself and are going to act from this different opinion. This option becomes possible only when the negative part has shifted and become a "something" that we are in relation to rather than identified with.

While these negative messages may still radically affect us, the important thing is that we stop having to act (or react) from them by sabotaging or working against ourselves. When we become aware of one of these unchanging places inside, its history and origin, whose voice it carries, why it feels the way it does, there is the experience of being set free from it, of seeing it and having a choice whether to act from it or not. No longer, however, are we ruled by our unconscious reaction to it.

Teri is a professional riding trainer who coaches some of the leading show riders in the United States. Before becoming a trainer, she had been a tremendously successful and well-respected rider herself. She came to me with a vague feeling of stress and agitation regarding her career. While her agitation was somewhat hard to pinpoint, one thing she knew for sure was that she felt utterly responsible for her students' performances and the results that followed. Teri had determined that it was up to her and her alone to make her students win in the ring. It was expected by the universe. Given that a number of her students were young, Teri was also certain that her students' parents expected her to be able to make their children win. She was thus failing the parents as well as herself (and the universe) when the child made a mistake. Even when she had expressed and demonstrated a particular skill with absolute clarity so that the student was able to execute it in training, still, if the student made an error in the show ring, it was Teri's error. She had not done her job because they had not done their job.

This was a particularly difficult problem when it came to less talented riders as it was Teri's task to be able to give them the talent that they did not possess. It was her responsibility to make everything go right even when it was entirely out of her control. No matter what went wrong, Teri was convinced that she was to blame. Ironically, this virtually ego-less woman could have been described as someone who felt that she was the only person in the world who could make anything happen. It wasn't as if she thought she took care of things so well or she felt any pride in her ability to get things done. Rather than a sense of power or confidence, hers was an experience of unbearable burden. For Teri, there was no reveling in the credit for a job well done. There was only the fear of being blamed for a job not done correctly. She was to blame until it got done right. When she sent a student off to compete, she stood by the side of the ring in a state of panic. Her job was never done. I understood her burden.

One Monday she showed up very upset. She had taken one of her students to an important horse show over the weekend. Everything had been done correctly leading up to the event. The horse appeared to be in perfect condition to do his job. The student was able to execute all the required tasks. Everything had been checked and re-checked. Nothing was spared; no shortcuts had been taken. The team was ready. Unfortunately, horses are not controllable, and when the horse got to the show grounds, he decided he wasn't going to do anything the girl asked. The animal was completely out of control for the entire competition. Nothing had gone according to plan. In a moment of exasperation, Teri's student had turned to her and wailed "Why is this happening?" Of course Teri had no way of knowing why the horse was misbehaving, but there was something about the girl's question that triggered a feeling of rage and helplessness in Teri.

When she came to me on Monday she was in tears. As we explored the experience of the weekend, the nucleus of Teri's problem became clearer, or to put it another way, the problem began to take on a more definite shape. So far in the treatment, we had talked about her being responsible for the outcome of all of her student's performances, but there was something in our discussion that hadn't yet hit it exactly right. There is a moment when you reach the core of a problem when you can feel a sense of relief, a sort of "Oh that's it" that happens in the body, an internal sigh. Until that Monday we hadn't gotten there.

Teri kept coming back to her student's question "Why is this happening?" She felt utterly responsible for having an answer that would make it clear and explain it to the girl. She had to know why this horse had behaved so out of character, but the fact was that she didn't know. There was no way to know. She had to know the unknowable. Teri was desperate. Thankfully, I was starting to understand her problem a bit better. It was clear that it wasn't enough for her to commit to investigating or trying to discover a possible answer over time. No, this internal place of hers felt that she had to have an answer right away, at the moment the question was posed. Regardless of the particular question at hand, she felt this all the time. Believe it or not, we were making progress. We were getting closer to the center of the problem. It was about having to have the answers, not later, but now. As we asked this part of her questions, we also came to discover that the part felt utterly alone and terrified. She couldn't and shouldn't have to ask for help from anyone. These were all important clues to the history of this place in her. The next step was to get to know what drove this place, what the underlying feeling of it was. At first the feeling was pressure and anxiety. As we went deeper into what sat under the anxiety we found that this place was being driven by fear. It was desperately afraid, terrified, of not having the answer. When we asked the place itself what it knew that made it so afraid, it told us that "no one would stick around if she didn't have the answer."

After finding this belief, Teri recounted a number of memories relating to her father. He was an emotionally brutal man who spoke to her only in riddles, always testing her to see if she was clever enough to figure out his questions, and thus deem her worthy of his love and attention. The only thing that mattered to him about Teri was that she could figure out and solve his riddles. He would quiz her every day on different topics and took great pleasure in her knowing the answers to his little games. He expressed no interest in the activities of her life, what she thought about or who she was.

She described the feeling of being with him much like she talked about her experience of teaching. What's more, her father continually ridiculed and humiliated those who didn't have the answers to his little games, including Teri's sister and brother. The father chose Teri as his favorite precisely because she was able to answer his questions. Teri cried as she talked about how her father had abandoned her brother and sister, dumping them because they were too stupid to know the answers. She had her father's love precisely because she could come up with the answers

Overcoming Negativity

without asking for help and, on the drop of a hat. She grew up knowing in no uncertain terms (albeit unconsciously) that her father would abandon her too on the day that she needed help or didn't know the answer.

Discovering what was at the core of "not having the answers" allowed for a big shift in Teri's internal experience. After seeing this until-now unformulated belief in herself, Teri could approach her student's questions with a broader perspective. The girl's question had triggered this old place of terror, one that her body had always carried and that had never healed. Not being able to find an answer for this student's question had launched Teri's body right into the experience of knowing that her father soon would begin humiliating her, casting her off as an idiot, and most terrifyingly, preparing to abandon her as he had her brother and sister. Despite it being 30 years later and an entirely different situation, this was precisely the trauma Teri's body was living when she walked into my office on that Monday morning. No time at all had lapsed for Teri's internal reality. This was what her body was living regardless of what her head knew to be the facts.

So how does knowing this help? When Teri is now asked a question to which she doesn't have the answer, she still feels a moment of terror and anxiety, but what's different is her reaction to those feelings. She can now recognize the place in her that was afraid of a very real thing, of being ridiculed and abandoned by her father. In so doing, she gently acknowledges what this place actually lived and suffered. Her emotional response to the anxiety that gets triggered is radically different, as is how she is then able to act or react.

Knowing about her core place, experiencing what her actual terror is about, frees Teri from feeling overwhelmed by the current situation. It is as if she can now say, "Oh yes, there's that place in me that feels so afraid because of Dad and having to come up with an answer for Dad." In so doing she can then see that her feelings of anxiety relate to that experience and not this student's question. Until there is an understanding of what the bigger issue or core experience is, we are helpless to these unconscious feelings and thus, end up reacting in a way that doesn't seem to fit the situation. It is the old place that has triggered our reaction and its intensity. Our body has a certain kind of memory; core experiences get cellularly logged in a specific way. Certain types of experiences get pooled together to form these core places that have a certain feel and experience in our bodies. New experiences can trip off these core places when the body senses something familiar, something that feels like the old place of hurt, as if the body were internally tasting or smelling something that it knew (and suffered) from before. It then begins reacting as if the two situations were the same.

Our body, for example, may get a sense that a particular conversation or disagreement we are having today reminds it of a whole history of humiliation. Despite the new experience having nothing to do with the past, we find ourselves yelling and becoming very upset because of those previous experiences of being made to feel like an idiot. It is right there, happening to us all over again. Whether the words are being said or not, our body still hears the same message from the past. Once we can see and know the core place and what the real trauma we're carrying is all about, make some room for the pain that *it* lived, we can then separate out the new experience for what it is and thus, the weight it really deserves. Discovering and experiencing the core place frees us to act consciously.

I have met a wide spectrum of negative places and beliefs and I have seen many of them heal and change. From my experience, our negative parts or places are, in most cases, more like suffering creatures than evil demons. These parts of us usually want to change. They don't want to feel as badly as they do. They don't want to be abandoned outside "the door" to suffer alone. They are suffering parts of ourselves that have not been properly tended to, not appropriately parented. Those that should have tended to them did not, and now we ourselves do not. This is the real tragedy. In our own care, they must encounter a new kind of treatment. We must view these parts of ourselves as wanting to be healed, wanting our attention so that they can feel differently. The idea is to go towards them, welcome them. These places offer us an opportunity to bring nurturing to ourselves. When a negative place feels heard and understood, when it is given the chance to tell its story, to bring its vague sense into focus, it will feel better and begin the process of healing.

The human organism, when given the right conditions, will move towards its own state of wellness. It seeks internal harmony. It is when we can offer *all* the parts of ourselves an open, non-judgmental ear and welcome shoulder that we most effectively provide the conditions that allow for our natural state of wellness to develop.*

*see Recommended Reading.

THINKING POSITIVE

As you think, so you become.

❧

*I*n several chapters I have examined the damaging impact of negative thoughts, but here I want to address the flip side, namely, the incredible benefits of positive thinking. I would guess that at this moment, having heard the time-worn term "positive thinking" for so many years, some of you may be put off. "Positive thinking" is so over-used it has little meaning left. But right now, make a choice to give positive thinking a fresh look, to approach it as if you had never heard of it, to really put on your "beginner's cap." Leave your cynicism at the gate and give me your full attention. If you are not ready to do this at this moment, skip this chapter and come back to it when you think you can.

I came late to the world of positive thinking. "What good are changing my thoughts if I still FEEL the same way?" was my question to the positive thinkers. Two things were clear to me in my "old" way of thinking.

1. If I thought it, I felt it. If I felt it, it was truth. If it was truth then it was something I could not control. Deductively then, if I thought it was out of my control.

2. A thought was caused by a feeling and/or belief I had about myself and this cause and effect relationship went only ONE way. Feelings had the power to change thoughts, but thoughts could not change feelings. (In the childhood "rock, scissors, paper" game, feelings definitely beat out thoughts.) There was a third thing that was clear to me at the time as well, namely, that anyone who ascribed to the idea of positive thinking should have his head examined!

ENERGY AT WORK

In the last chapter I discussed the idea that every thought has a story, a past, an internally logical reason for feeling the way it does. This is true. This is not to say however, that there isn't also something helpful in using positive thinking as an adjunct to exploring these negative parts. In moments of performance, it is not always possible to do this deeper kind of exploring. So too, there are negative thoughts that show up purely out of habit, even after we understand and feel compassion for the part of us that is doing the reasoning. Certain negative thoughts we don't even believe anymore; they are just there, like a faulty wiring switch that can get tripped off. There is a word in Sanskrit for habitual thoughts, *Samskara*. *Samskara* literally means "groove in the mind" (as in a phonograph record). The word is used to describe a thought that has become a "rut," a hole into which we are inclined to fall again and again. As the habitual thought or groove gets deeper, it becomes more difficult to avoid, and so we stumble in more often, deepening the hole and worsening our future chances of escaping it. Thoughts that we think habitually get more and more ingrained in our minds until it no longer matters whether we believe them. We fall into them simply because they're there, waiting for us.

A rider who constantly thinks and worries about her horse tripping and falling before a jump will soon find herself tumbling from a stumbling beast. So too, we all know about the "placebo effect" in science. By simply thinking that he is getting healthier, a patient can actually make his body be healthier, often reversing otherwise "unstoppable" disease processes. Our thoughts have energy; they *are* energy. When we think, we release that energy into the universe and, quite literally, make things happen. It makes sense then, that if we can shape our internal world, we should be able to create our external or "concrete" reality as well. At every moment of our lives, we are creating the "state" in which we exist. If we are thinking and feeling negativity, we are creating a negative existence for ourselves in that moment; we are living negativity. Imagine that you were sculpting with a mound of clay that was speckled with shards of glass; no matter how talented an artist you were, the chances would be slim that anything you created could come out "smooth" and without the power to cut you. So too, with an internal environment made of negativity, it is difficult and improbable that you could create anything positive for your life.

If every time we face a difficult challenge, we think, "I'm ruined now," we most certainly will be. If, however, we can notice our thought and the fact that we are telling ourselves this, then we can do something proactive and replace that thought with words like, "The tougher it gets the better I get" or "I will rally for the challenge" or "I have done this before and will do it again." Whatever works. The point is that while a part of us may (or may not) still believe that we're ruined, positive words can do some damage control, balancing and counteracting the negative thought, generating strong positive energy where there was only the negative. So too, when inserting a positive thought into one of these negative grooves, at the very least we suggest the possibility that the reality we're assuming is not the only possible reality for our lives. We bring in the voice of reason where there has been only distortion. The mere suggestion of a different reality in and of itself is beneficial.

In order to create new, more positive grooves in your mind (feelings and thoughts that support and encourage you), you must be willing to start from a place of discomfort, to try on new ways of seeing your world. Before the new thoughts have trickled down into beliefs, each attempt at "thinking positively" will feel like trying on a hat made of words. It will (and should) feel awkward. If you keep at it, rigorously noticing and replacing each habitually negative thought with a habitually positive one, gradually, your new, more positive hat can actually melt into your own head.

In addition, use your body. It may sound strange, but when we carry ourselves "confidently," we dramatically increase the chances of becoming confident. Like the act of thinking positive thoughts, the simple act of moving your body with confidence (no matter how many John Wayne movies you have to watch to get it right) will change your body's chemistry.

Whether we're faking it or not is meaningless. Energy and confidence are released into our system regardless of whether our mind has "agreed," as of yet, to come along for the ride. When you carry your body differently, your body *feels* differently. New experiences are immediately possible.

YOU WIN SOME, YOU LOSE SOME

In some cases (often with young performers) exploring the beliefs, experiences and feelings of the self-critical part of the self is not possible, and thus, a positive approach can be useful. Having worked with Samantha for some months, I knew that attempting to get to know or hear from the part of her that judged her imperfection to be despicable and unacceptable was not yet an option. I therefore proceeded with a different approach.

"So let me get this straight," Samantha said, looking perplexed with her hands on her tiny hips. "I'm supposed to tell myself that I'm happy when I fall off the beam?"

"Let's get one thing straight," I said without answering her question, "Today, if you were to fall off the beam, would you hate yourself?"

"Yes," she nodded strongly.

"And for how long would you hate yourself?"

"A couple days, maybe."

"OK, so every time you fall off the beam, you live two really crummy days. Would it be fair to say that two days of your life are ruined?"

"Uh huh," she agreed cheerfully, conspicuously rejecting the path where I was heading.

"Would you like to change this?"

"I'd like to fall off the beam less," she said, adeptly dodging my help once again.

"What if for right now you could only control the effect that falling HAS on you and not the falling itself. In that case, would you like to not feel so bad when it happens?"

"I guess so," she reluctantly agreed, no doubt fearing what many performers do, namely, that my goal is to teach them how to get comfortable with failure.

"It's not about being happy to fall off the beam," I consoled her. "But rather, instead of focusing on the terrible, worthless failure that you are because of your fall, what if you were to shift your focus and think about all the learning that this fall will make possible, how this fall offers you the opportunity to grow as an athlete, to really stretch and get better."

"Aren't I training myself to want to fall then? I mean, aren't I making falling a good thing? No matter what, falling has to be dreaded. It isn't a good thing," she reprimanded me, no longer able to mask her irritation.

"You are never going to want to fall, of that you are not in danger. But by simply changing your thoughts from negative to positive when you do fall (which from time to time is inevitable), you might be able to shave off one of those two days of hopelessness. You might even be able to live in a different "world" altogether for those two days. How does that sound?" She didn't answer.

As I saw it, I had two major problems in working with this young athlete, and specifically, her thinking habits. First, in her mind, falling was not an "inevitable," imperfection, not yet a "given," and thus my basic premise was not only rejected, but deeply bothersome to her. Secondly (and perhaps more importantly), the two days that were "lost" each time she stumbled were, in her estimation, appropriate punishment for the crime of imperfection. Self-torture was the inevitable, not falling. Samantha was not yet willing to let go of her thoughts and so we moved on.

The negative thoughts triggered by failure are often the most stubborn and hardest to change. After a lifetime of imperfection, the habits are strong, the ruts very deep. Because you believe so intensely in what the negative thoughts are telling you about yourself, it would seem contradictory to insert any kind of positive thought. Also, there is the fear that by thinking positive and kind thoughts in the face of imperfection, you will be encouraging that imperfection, increasing your chances of getting sloppy. No matter how violently the negative thoughts grab hold or how desperately the positive ones try to flee, stick with it. Like the negative habits, your positive habits (and beliefs) will grow strong if given the chance. Be rigorous. Give them the chance.

A client once asked me the following: "If I could surgically remove one and only one negative thought from my brain, literally take it out with a scalpel, which thought would you suggest I target?" It was an odd question, but I answered instantly without considering its oddness. "The thought I would remove (and it would be difficult to capture it entirely because, like a cancer, it mutates into so many different forms), but it would be the thought that says 'My life *shouldn't* be this way or 'is not *supposed* to be this way.' Needless to say, this is not a thought we often have when things are going smoothly or "our way." The 'it is not supposed to be this way' thought crops up when situations are uncomfortable or painful. So in fact, the underlying thought is 'My life *shouldn't* be so hard.'

Of all the thoughts we think as humans, this is the one that creates the most suffering. In fact, this thought creates more suffering than most anything we experience in life. For if your life is supposed to be different and better, then there is a wonderful existence continually eluding you, a "place in the sun" with your name on it, if you could only figure out how to get there. But you can't. If this is indeed the case, then you are either the victim of some terrible fate or a hopeless failure, unable to turn your life into the fun, easy, and enjoyable trip that it is supposed to be (and no doubt everyone else is enjoying). This thought can only create frustration, anger and depression.

Your place in the sun exists, but it rains there too. Lesson number one: performance is *not* easy. Lesson number two (the more important one): performance is *not supposed* to be easy. Although this may sound depressing, it can be quite relieving and liberating. More often than not, it is not the specific problem or difficulty you're facing that causes the bulk of pain in your life, but rather the idea that it is supposed to be some other way, namely, better. When you are able to relieve yourself of this thought, you are left simply with the problem itself and this is always a far less daunting opponent. If "it's not supposed to be easy" then you are simply experiencing "what is supposed to be" at any given moment. As a result, you need not waste so much time and energy (in the form of despair) on "how it should be" or "what you're missing." You are free to get on with the process of living the life that actually IS yours, the life that IS at this moment.

PARENTS

It is up to you to decide who you are.
Is it your turn to live yet?

❦

W hen Karen first came to see me, she was conflicted
about her own success. Despite possessing a lot of
talent, she was constantly sabotaging her progress
while talking about how much she hated being trapped in a
mediocre life. She felt that the sad reality of her parents'
lives prevented her from living the life she desired. She
wondered how her life could mean something to her when
her father's life never meant anything to him. How could she
feel passion when he spent his whole life trying to find it?
How could she be happy when her mother never was? Neither
one of her parents could make their lives what they wanted,
and now she was faced with the decision of how to design her
own life. Did she have to deny herself, to make her life like
theirs, or could she live a different and better kind of
existence? Would that be unfair? The truth was, they were

not able to make their lives better—she was. They probably would not have chosen to live the way they did but did that mean that she would have to continue suffering? Would her happiness be punishment for their failure, humiliation for what they could not do?

On the other hand, was it about her not wanting to face her disappointment in *them*, to look at who her parents really were (in all their humanness). Did they not fail *her* with their unhappiness? And then again, she felt afraid to leave them, to make herself different. Her own stuckness kept her from having to rub their 'loss' in their faces. So too, it saved her from having to accept her parents' limitations and suffering and thus to accept her own separateness. She was not like them. But if she was not like and *with* them, then was she not out there on her own in the universe, to make her life whatever it could be? As she surmised, "I suppose, up until now, it's been easier and less scary to let my life, disappointing or not, be determined by my past, to stay close to home, inside the womb, WITH them and not separate, not on my own with the responsibility for my life in my own hands." These are tough tasks. Is your own life important enough to face the challenge?

Parents are a complicated topic (to state the obvious). How does your relationship with your parents affect your success? How does it impact your willingness or *unwilling-ness* to let that success happen. There is a specific *you* who exists in relationship to your parents. Given this, it may be necessary to re-construct this relationship (even if it is just in your mind) in order for you to create a different and successful you. Building a new relationship between you and your parents is primarily an internal process and one that can go on regardless of whether your parents are alive or not. The idea is to develop your own image of yourself, an image that is based on what *you* believe to be true about yourself, an image that may be very different from what your parents believed.

GROWING PAINS

Allowing yourself to succeed means that you have to create a new place for yourself in relation to your parents, letting go of the disappointment and damage that occurred in the past and the *you* who was associated with that damage. It is up to the adult you to create a new life for yourself based on who you are *now*, regardless of who you felt like as a child or who your family continues to see you as. It is about moving forward in your life and creating something fresh, something based on the person *you* know you are and *can be*.

So how do you do this? First, you must learn to stop using your present as a way of correcting or avenging what happened in your past. Your parents probably failed you. Most do, regardless of whether they try their best or not. But more importantly, by refusing to allow yourself to succeed here in the present, you are failing yourself. We can't do anything about what your parents did, but we can do something about what you are doing. By failing, you may be (unknowingly) trying to prove to your parents (and yourself) how thoroughly they ruined your life, how badly they hurt you. In your system, success would mean letting them off the hook, forgiving them for what they did to you. After all, if you were to actually be happy or become a success, how bad could they really have been as parents?

Unfortunately, if your goal is to evoke your parents' guilt, this is a tough way to achieve it. Continuing to sacrifice your own potential in an effort to *punish* your parents does only one thing, it keeps *you* unhappy. Most likely, the characters from your past have moved on with their lives. Even if you believe that they are suffering by way of your unhappiness, is it really worth being unhappy for? Move on. Turn your attention to your own life. Failure is revenge only on yourself.

FROM REACTION TO ACTION

You may never totally forgive your parents, that's OK. What is *not* OK is for you to continue blaming the past for your present. It is the blame that takes your focus *off* your present life and thus keeps you from changing that life. It is the blame that keeps you stagnant, locked in this cycle of failure. In order to break free, you must first truly believe that this is *your* life and not your parents'. It is now up to you to determine what this life will hold. Letting go of the past is about shifting from a life of reaction to one of action. Living in continual reaction makes a genuine life impossible. After all, the script is not written by you but dictated by those who you're still trying to change or enlighten.

Did your parents offer you what you wanted or needed when you were a child? If the answer was "no," then why are you choosing to spend your *now* with them still as your keepers? As a child, you had to endure certain things. You had no choices. News flash: the baby-sitters have all gone home; you can stay up as late as you want, eat all the cookies in the cookie jar. Your life waits for you like a fresh canvas. Live this now and let the past be over.

LEAVING HOME

And what about your parents' lives? Were *they* happy, fulfilled, satisfied? If not, your own success may leave you feeling not only different and separate, but guilty. Your happiness may translate into abandoning them, leaving them to suffer alone. By failing in your own life, you refrain from leaving them behind; you are saved from having to really look at your parents' suffering. Success would provide you with a different kind of life from which to view them. Joining them in their suffering, on the other hand, keeps you from having to make that break, to separate and see them from the outside. In holding yourself back and postponing your life, you attempt to save your parents; their suffering is not so intolerable if you are all in it together. *Your* failure changes the experience from one of sadness (for them) to one of anger and frustration for you. Simultaneously, there is relief in knowing that you can bear the same suffering as your parents, thereby making their pain less overwhelming.

This scenario must eventually become tiresome. It takes a lot of work to keep throwing your life away in an effort to save theirs. Your life is happening (or passing) regardless of whether you choose to pay attention to it. Either you create something different for yourself or you will have wasted your own existence in a futile effort to save theirs. Why are you not entitled to a life? Why is your life's work to save theirs? Remind yourself, these are *your* parents, they were supposed to be there to help you. Believe it or not, *you* were and are supposed to *get* something from them. *You* deserve to have been parented. If this didn't happen then you are entitled to mourn, but don't waste any more time on trying to change what has already happened. Don't dedicate any more of your own power and energy to their failure. Why are they not responsible for their own lives? Are you not responsible for yours? Time goes by fast. The time has come for you to *forgive* yourself for having a good life even if their lives were not.

If you give yourself the life your parents couldn't give themselves, go places they could not, who will be *your* parents? Parents are supposed to remain forever "above" their children. Surpassing your parents removes any hope of remaining a child. Consequently, you must accept your role as an adult in the world and relinquish the protection and safety of your unending childhood. By giving yourself the life you deserve, it may feel as if you are leaving your parents behind, venturing forward alone into an unknown world. The process requires a more honest vision of who your parents are as people, their limitations, disappointments and suffering. Getting over your parents and into your own life is an intensely real and difficult process.

From a session with Karen:

It's enough now. I have yet to live my own life and that hasn't stopped the earth from going around the sun. And by the way, I'm ready to have those thirty years back now, now that I'm willing to treat my own life with respect, ready to value my own choices and existence. Guess what, no one's listening and no one cares. It's only me that needs to care. I've lived my life through a keyhole instead of with the door open. But that time is gone, the longer I lament it, the more time I waste.

Ironically, allowing yourself to succeed is the best thing you can do for your parents; your success gives them a new person to relate to and thus the potential for a new way of being themselves. By changing yourself (which is all you can change) you break the cycle of despair and not only offer a new example to them, but cease in enabling the pattern of stagnation.

THE CRUEL TRUTH

And then there is the critical parent. In addition to its other "perks," being the child of an intensely critical parent can create a strong resistance to success. But what if your parents didn't call you names, didn't yell at you at all? Remember, criticism comes in many forms, some of it very subtle. It need not arrive in the standard name-calling or "You'll never amount to anything" variety. Some of the most insidious forms of criticism are delivered in the less obvious but no-less damaging style of consistent, but "quiet" undermining and belittling of spirit.

> **A rider:** *When I succeed in any way, the response I hear from my mother is 'That's great. (pause) How did that happen?' I wonder what message I received from that kind of "support."*

If one or both of your parents were very critical, it may be inconceivable for you to believe that *you* could succeed, to imagine yourself as a success. To actualize your talent, that which has been unrecognized and rejected, would be to prove this critical parent wrong. Your success would illuminate the truth, namely, that such criticism was misguided, fictional and unkind. While self-sabotage may mean giving up a satisfying life, its alternative, accepting who your parents really were and how unfairly they may have treated you, can feel like a far worse punishment.

By choosing to stay stuck, you are acknowledging that it is in fact less painful for you to "amount to nothing" and thus, prove your parents right, than become something and confront their cruelty. Getting in your own way is a way of preventing yourself from ever knowing what it would be like to face the contradiction between who your parents told you you were and who you really are.

In order to create a new kind of life, you must take the risk and experience the pain of this unknown. Eventually you may even reach a place of compassion for yourself—compassion for the you who was misjudged and for the life you have thus far deprived yourself.

10

THE COMPETITION

Those you love and hate, all of them are only you.
Do you deserve your own attention?

"It's always about them," explained Caroline, a
35-year-old equestrian who had been competing since
she was 12. On this particular day, she sounded defeated
and exhausted from her struggle. "No matter how much
success I earn, it never sinks in, I still just have to beat
them."

"Who is this them?" I asked.

"*Them* are the players for whom it could really happen,
the ones who if it happened for, it would be real. I'm never
the *one*," she went on, raising her hands over her head to
convey what she meant by the *one*. "It's never real when it
happens for me. I've got to fend them off, over and over and
over...every horse show they start out above me in my mind,
surrounding me, trying to destroy me. And if I don't destroy

them first... It's never about my success, just keeping them from making a gigantic fool of me. Can you imagine? It's so pathetic. Will this ever end? Will it ever be fun? I mean, will I ever get to enjoy any of it, any of my accomplishments?"

The road to the top is crowded. The path of greatness demands one important skill: the ability to step into your own attention, to pull your focus away from the pack and place it in and on yourself. Whatever (or whoever) owns your attention, owns your power and your rights. Only one thing: your task, has the right to inhabit the center of your own attention.

Ask yourself, why is it that your competitors deserve to occupy your attention, while *you* on the other hand, do not? What assumptions do you make about your competitors that thereby award them this privilege? Are you convinced that your competitors are inherently more legitimate than you, that their lives are valuable (as opposed to your own)? This problem has nothing to do with your competition or their lives and everything to do with you and your life. It is in your perception of your own life versus your perception of their lives that the difference exists, not the lives themselves. Although you are certain that one exists, in fact there is *no* life you could be living that would provide you with the imagined legitimacy you ascribe to your competitors. When you can make your own life mean something *to you*, what these others are doing ceases to be a source of great interest or value.

ENVY

Throughout history, envy has traditionally been considered an ugly emotion. Its color is green, symbolizing jaundice and illness. Envy is linked to aggression, ill-will, deceit, malice and bad sportsmanship. What is considered so ugly about envy is that it is not only about wanting to have what you are lacking, but wanting others *not* to have it. So too, it is an emotion that generates shame; it puts you below someone else and thus acts as an injury to your ego. As Chaucer said, "It is certain that envy is the worst sin that is; for all other sins are sins only against one virtue, whereas envy is against all goodness."

Webster's dictionary defines envy as "pain or discontent excited by another's superiority or success." The verb to envy means to begrudge or covet what another has. What is present in each of these definitions? "Another." Envy is about an *other*. Envy makes you feel small and shrunken as a result of what you perceive to be another's bigness. You want what they have so you stare at it, think about it, obsess over it. You become so involved in what this other has that you forget that you are there at all. You disappear into the shadows of the very light you are shining on that object of envy. You create your own absence.

No matter how well we understand it however, envy is not easy to control. The problem with envy is that once you're in it, you're *in* it. Envy is like a raging sea storm, it grabs hold of and consumes you. It is difficult to look at envy while you're riding its waters. It is important, therefore, to take advantage of the time when the internal sea is calm. This is the time when you can recognize your own value without comparing yourself. What role is envy playing in your life? What do you get by keeping it alive? Do you entertain the emotion as a way of denigrating yourself, making yourself invisible, rejecting your own position? Does this provide some sort of relief? Is this the way things are "supposed" to be? Remember, envy makes the game about others; as long as you are involved in envy the game is never about you. No matter what you accomplish, you simply don't matter as much as they do.

In truth, others' accomplishments have nothing to do with your success. How can I say this, you ask? If they win, you lose—does this not relate to your success? *It does not.* You don't lose because they win. You lose because you lose. The only element of their success that impacts negatively on you is the amount of time and energy you invest (and waste) in focusing on it. The more time you spend involved in their being better than you, the more you ensure their superiority. Your envy works to strengthen the very thing you fear and despise. Your competitors would thank you profusely were they to know how much power you are awarding them, how dedicated you are to helping their cause. They are in the plum position of not only having their own attention working for them, but yours as well. What would happen if you placed all of that attention and energy on yourself and your task? Could you stand it?

Consider something you once coveted—a position, title, accomplishment, trait, person, possession—anything that you intensely wanted and now have. Remember how desperately you wanted that thing? And now that you have it, do you honor its presence with the same intensity and desperation you did its absence? Or, once in your possession, has it fallen to the ranks of the ordinary? Rest assured, those things on *today's* can't-live-your-life-without list will seem mundane once you have them. The objects of envy, in and of themselves, are *not* what you are craving. The most appealing aspect of these objects is that *you* don't have them (or at least don't perceive yourself to have them). These "things" thus offer you the chance for a different life, a different you, the eternal goal. The carrot on the end of the stick must change each time you reach it and discover that it is only a carrot and still *you* who is holding it. It is the *not having* it that allows you to infuse it with such hope, delude yourself with the conviction that *it* is the something that will finally give you the life you're supposed to be living. Once again, think back to the time before you had *it*, when you were convinced that if you ever did get *it*, your life would be complete, different, full, better. Now that you have *it*, is your life completely different? Completely satisfying? Completely perfect? The challenge is in finding what you want within the walls of your own self. Those aspects of your competitor that you envy so intensely are all within you. Either you are ignoring them or you simply haven't yet given them the attention they need to develop.

Jon is a 55-year-old competitive sailboat racer who had spent his whole life consumed with what others had and what he didn't. He wanted their boats, their wives, their names, their clothes, in short, their lives. And then one day he showed up with a different expression on his face, a less tormented one. I asked him about it and he remarked that he had stumbled onto a new feeling, one that gave him a good deal of relief. "It's like this," he said, smiling, "the others to whom I devote so much time, *I can't be them,* no matter how much time I spend staring at them and thinking about what they have. This life that I envy, that occupies all of my thinking, it's always going to be theirs. I cannot live that life no matter how badly I want it. This is not to say that my life can't contain those things that I want—OK maybe not Callahan's wife—but that spectacular guy in that spectacular boat with that spectacular job, wife, family, body and mind, *his* life will never be mine."

There is only one life that you will ever be able to inhabit; only one mind, body and spirit that you will ever possess. These are *your* materials—get to work with what you've got.

THE CHOSEN PEOPLE

As you consider envy, also become aware of your tendency to turn certain performers into demi-Gods. The demi-Gods are those who, in your eyes, have no problems and live perfect lives. These are the competitors you consider to be the *real* thing, those that define and embody your passion. They *are* it. You probably have elaborate fantasies and assumptions about these folks without having had any real contact with them. This idolatry is very different than envy. While envy usually implies a degree of concrete competitiveness, idolatry does not. Demi-Gods play in a different universe than you. They are so *real* as to become unreal, illusions. They are no longer just people, but myths. As a different species than you, they exist outside your realm of envy. Who is on your list? What qualities do you assign these folks? For one of my clients, "they" are always confident, never nervous. For another, "they" never blame or doubt themselves. And still another, "they" never make mistakes at all, never have to learn and are simply born winning. By holding these demi-Gods in a place above you, as completely different and separate from you, you keep *your* un-realness and childishness alive. You cannot become a serious competitor in your own mind as long as these "real" players remain so different from you.

Make an effort to spend some time with your demi-gods. Ask one to lunch, have a conversation with her. Spend some actual (as opposed to fantasy) time with your example of "realness." Chances are, you will see her humanness, her just-like-you-ness. You may discover that you are more like her than you imagine. That inherently special quality you assign to her that awards her *real* status, is *not* a quality of hers at all. It is an aspect of *your* mind. When these so-different-than-you competitors can become regular people, when you can see yourself in the same game as them, you will be on your way to shattering your own illusion of falseness and invisibility.

LOOKING DOWN

You may notice that different issues arise depending on what level competitor you are facing. Performers who are below you "on the ladder" are often responsible for generating the fiercest of emotions. These are the ones to whom you must constantly prove your superiority, those that must be destroyed in order for you to prove your "place."

A figure skater:

Their position below me provides me with a retort to my internal audience. At least I am better than them; the critics within me can't disagree with that. Being better than someone else means that I must have some minimal validity, that at least I must exist as a competitor.

Is the presence of such competitors distracting for you? Do they take you out of your task, make it difficult for you to perform up to your true potential? Do you find yourself thinking about how you must crush them as opposed to concentrating on your own performance? Are you constantly trying *not* to screw up, *not* to prove them and your own internal audience "right" about you? Does it feel as if such competitors are always gathering evidence to confirm that you're not the real thing? Once again, the real problem is not them, but *you*. You are involved in proving who you are *not* as opposed to being who you are. In this system, your competitors create and own *your* experience. Neither your success nor your passion can even belong to you; your competitors dictate your experience.

There is another way. Relief from this roller coaster of annihilation comes when you can learn to define yourself by *who* you are as opposed to *where* you are in relation to others, to exist on your own without relying on someone else's position above or below you to determine your self-image. A "relative" you cannot sustain any real confidence. With comparison as your sole source of meaning, your self-image will forever be at the mercy of others' failure (which you can't control) and your own perfection (which is not possible). Your self-image must become self-sufficient. It is only you who must be convinced of your talent and only you who can allow yourself to step into the role of the experienced performer you have become. Start paying attention to yourself!

HAPPY HALLOWEEN

No one can steal your experience from you but you. These competitors to whom you award so much power and attention are nothing more than masks under which to hide your own self-destructive instincts. It's just you hiding behind those enemy mugs. In and of themselves, your competitors possess no power over you; they are irrelevant. The power you assign to them is nothing more than *your* disowned power projected onto them. Their faces, like Halloween masks, merely shield the devaluing and destructive aspects of yourself, your internal demons. Do not be fooled, you and the voices of your past are behind these masks. Your competitors will cease being a threat when you stop handing them your sword. The whole game is between you and you—everything and everyone else is just distraction. You're it.

Every so often it is important to remind yourself that for those performers below you, *you* are the object of *their* envy. This may be difficult to imagine, that you could be someone to envy, that anyone could think of you as important or someone they would like to be. Consider your image of those above you and remind yourself that this is precisely the way that these up-and-comers view *you*. No matter what you read into their glances, you can be sure that they are seeing you as the performer who, first and foremost, is above them. Remember this as you are employing them to humiliate yourself. The truth is, they want what you have. *Imagine that*! Those below you are not expecting you to fail. You are.

THE GENUINE ARTICLE

Become aware of the cycle of invalidation you unleash on yourself when in the company of your competitors. Do you distrust your own legitimacy and "place" even more when in their presence? Do you question whether your legitimacy and belonging will be obvious enough *to them*? Do you find yourself desperately trying to *prove* your own importance and membership? Must they believe it before it can feel real to you? Ironically, this proving forces you to sacrifice the very comfort and naturalness you're so desperately trying to demonstrate. You step outside the self that *is* real in order to create a false self that will *appear* real. The problem is that you already *are* real. Authenticity is *within* you; it is only you who doesn't believe it. Besides wasting a lot of energy, "playing real" has an even more damaging effect. Namely, your competitors succeed at turning you into exactly the impostor, the unreal phantom, you are trying so hard to prove you're not. Their power to do this to you then intensifies your anger and humiliation, furthering your belief that you will never be a member of the real club.

Ironically, by doing *nothing* other than being yourself, you unmistakably demonstrate your authenticity and place. Creating authenticity is an oxymoron. The instant you start trying to prove your place, that place will disappear; you will have lost the un-self-conscious nature that is the essence of authenticity. Trust your realness; it will be there when you stop looking for it. It will *be* when you stop trying to create it.

A PLACE TO BE

A swimmer writes:

> How dare they get to have my sport. I'm the real swimmer when it comes to actual skill and success, and yet inside they are the ones who identify themselves as swimmers. This identity then makes them feel even more special and entitled. I have been swimming so much longer than most of them, and yet they get to be proud of it, to be it. I suppose I should use the words "choose to" as opposed to "get to," but the element of choice escapes me. Until recently I was unable even to accept my role as a swimmer. And to think, I'm the one who can actually swim, the one who can do the thing that the title implies!
>
> I feel no sense of generosity, of wanting to share what is mine. I am just now able to give myself a place

in this sport. Having disowned my passion for so long makes their invasion that much more painful and disruptive. I just got here. More accurately, I've been here a long time in body, but it's just now that my spirit has arrived. It's too soon for these others (who are less skilled) to invade my new place with their assumed sense of ownership and entitlement. Looking at the pride and ease with which they take themselves and their passion seriously, I am face to face with my own very different experience. How brutally I have abandoned and rejected myself, how I have sought to destroy all that was me or my passion. I have had to earn my membership through undeniable skill and public success. When the rest of the world knew of it and approved, it was real. I could belong. Even then, I didn't get to fully embody my place; it felt tenuous, as if it could be stolen with one error or defeat. The fact that it was me and my passion implied nothing and certainly did not award that me or that passion with any inherent meaning or value. If anything, the fact that it was me made the fight for meaning and membership that much more grueling.

This swimmer, Katherine, is mesmerized by how certain competitors can accept and create a "place" for themselves *inside* and separate from whatever goes on in competition. For her, acceptance and legitimacy rely solely on how well she performs; her "place" is determined by external validation alone. This happens because there is no place for Katherine inside Katherine. She offers no home for herself within her own being. Consequently, she must look for something on the outside to offer her that place of acceptance and legitimacy. Believe it or not, there is a you that exists separate from all the external positioning. Becoming a success depends on finding *this* you. This is the you who will live your personal best (to say nothing of a satisfying life).

KILLER INSTINCT

"So what is this thing called killer instinct anyway? I know that I want to win, but I'm not so sure that I feel murderous about it. My coach is always talking about this killer instinct thing. Do I need it to succeed? And does the fact that I don't know if I have it already imply that I don't?"

Must this young competitor crave the physical annihilation of her competitors in order to win? The answer is no. However, had she asked me if there were a particular drive that she did need in order to succeed, one that she couldn't do without, I would have answered yes.

The necessary drive is defined by the desire and the willingness to get what you want *even* when getting what you want means depriving others of what they want. In sport, when you win, someone else loses. In performance, if you get the part, someone else does not. It is not enough to just want to win, you must be willing to have your competitors lose. Winning does not imply that you are a better person, it simply means that on this particular day you were the better competitor, yours the better game.

There is no room for *guilt* at the top. Guilt is a wet blanket that puts out your competitive fire and dismantles your drive. Winning is nothing to be guilty about. You win, not because fate chooses you as the victor but because *you* earn it.

Competition is not a party, there is no shared goal. There is no room for generosity once the competition begins. Your opponents want to win; they want to beat *you*. Why are you not allowed to want to win?

BE AGGRESSIVE

Being nice has nothing to do with succeeding. You can be nice and get what you want too. The two are not mutually exclusive. What you cannot do, however, is be the "good" girl (or boy) while on the court. You can be as "good" as you want up until the time the first ball is served. From then on, the rules change. "Good" now means working for yourself. You are not on that court to make everyone *else* happy, you are there to serve your *own* needs. Can you own your own desire? Can you honor what *you* want? Are you willing to give life to your more aggressive instincts?

You are not only entitled to, but if you want to win, dependent upon your aggressive urges. You need not apologize for this aspect of yourself. It is something to be celebrated. Aggression is *fuel* for your competitive force. If you want to win, you must be willing to take the risk that it is to re-activate these "unacceptable" instincts, these drives that society has asked you to deny.

YOU AS VICTOR

When you separate your *winning* from your opponents' *losing*, the former being acceptable, the latter not, you dilute your own power. Attempting to distinguish between the "good" and "bad" aspects of competition, your unconscious remains ever-aware of the guilt you associate with making others lose. As a result, you are inhibited from fully honoring your passion to succeed. You cannot pursue your desire as long as you are trying to put the "dark side" of that desire to sleep. By attempting to make two fires out of what is one, you *split* your passion. Throwing water on what you perceive to be the forbidden flame, you unknowingly dampen your competitive fire. You need all of that fire to reach your best.

It is not necessary to derive pleasure from seeing your opponent defeated. It is necessary, however, to get comfortable with your power and your *right* to make others lose. Making others lose is part of winning. If you perform better, then you deserve to be the winner. Winning is not selfish. You are not asking for anything to which you are not entitled. To be the victor does *not* mean that you have killed your opponent. Victory simply means that, as of this day, you are the better performer and thus deserve to reap the benefits of your superior work.

I have just written several pages about our right, as performers, to make others lose, to reap the benefits of our superior work, to celebrate our own aggression, if you will. It is important to note, however, that while this is all true, I don't believe that by winning, we actually make anyone else lose. We cannot make another lose—we can only make ourselves win. We are each responsible for our own fate. If our competitor has lost, he has lost because of just that, because *he* lost, *not* because we won. Winning and losing are isolated events—they exist within the same context, but they happen on their own. To lose is an active verb for a reason. Winning and losing do not depend upon each other to exist although they are often misperceived in this way. We can feel the right to win without feeling that we are responsible for another's losing. He who loses is solely responsible for that losing performance. It is each competitor's responsibility to deliver a performance worthy of victory. In this regard, we can never really beat anyone. They beat themselves. We can win, they can lose, but the two are entirely distinct events.

11

THE ZONE

*To experience new oceans
you must be willing to lose sight of the shore.*

∽

PRESENCE

*R*iding is the place in my life into which I can completely lose myself. As I write this, I realize that the word lose sounds frightening to me. What am I losing, I wonder. This is not the kind of losing that happens with distraction or escape. It is an aware and joyful loss. When I am riding I am more there; it is me in a different but more magnified form. I let go of the judgments and thoughts that perpetually separate me from and dilute my experiences. I am transformed into a more pure and whole form, totally focused without any sense of time. It is the only time in my life when I am totally in what I am doing and not trying to be somewhere else. It is true presence without mind-presence, a state of profound *awareness without the awareness of that awareness. "Flow" is a state of being in which the confines of me and my mortal mind cease to exist. It is the closest I get to immortality, a sense of complete freedom from the limitations of mortality, the truest freedom I have ever known.*

By now, you have probably heard about, and hopefully, experienced such aspects of the "zone" as are described here. Much has been written about "the zone" in recent years, so much in fact that "the zone" is now a pop phrase used to describe any experience in which one feels totally involved and alive. The zone is indeed a sacred and wonderful place, and yet there is an element of this place that is not discussed. Not surprisingly, it is precisely this element which can create fear and keep you from accessing your full potential.

WHERE AM I?

It is not the zone itself or being *in* it that is frightening. Rather, it is the idea of *getting* there, passing into this sacred place and thereby *leaving* and letting go of where and who you are now that can create terror. Getting into a new state of being requires leaving the old one and this means leaving the old *you*. Change creates fear. To reach the zone, you must let go of the self you know, the one you are in right now; you must give up the mind that is "aware" of and busy keeping tabs on your life. The process is a bit like agreeing to embark upon a journey on which you know *you* (or at least the you of this moment) will disappear. The flow experience creates a kind of you-less existence. The *you* who is a distinct and isolated entity disappears, which is precisely why you are able to join the experience so fully. *You* are not there to get in its way. Journeying into that unknown is taking a risk; it is agreeing to give up the clearly defined *you* who watches your life from that safe and separate place in your mind. The zone is about more than just becoming one with your craft, it is about losing yourself. The prospect of losing the self you know is frightening, after all, it is this soon-to-be-lost mind which is judging the safety of this journey.

From the outside, the prospect of letting go of yourself may sound frightening, like agreeing to your own death. No matter how many times you move in and out of the zone, each time you approach it, it may feel as if you are about to plunge into nothingness. Indeed, the flow experience can involve a kind of mini-death. Ironically, the feelings of loss usually appear as you re-enter your thinking, "aware" self. Suddenly, upon coming out of flow and back into your "head," you realize that you have been somewhere and someone else, simultaneously nowhere and everywhere. You are back in that known place, the you who is distinct from your experience. And yet that other, perhaps more authentic you who is not aware of her separateness, who's outline was more like a gas than a solid, she is gone again. Which *you* has suffered the mini-death?

Glancing at your watch to find that an entire day has passed without your "knowing" or noticing is both exhilarating and terrifying. What if this were to happen with your whole life? What if your mind's "awareness" never returned from the zone? What if your life happened without your mind being able to watch it, without your being "aware" of it, without being able to step outside and look at it? Is it only in looking at your life that you feel it or *you* exists?

Ironically, I feel most alive when I am not "there" in the normal sense. Right at this moment, I think of myself as being present precisely because my mind can sense where I begin and end. In those moments of total presence, my mind is not at all present, or at least I don't feel its presence. I am not an identifiable being, there is no I. What irony lurks in the term "mindful." Supposedly mindfulness is the goal, and yet I am most full when my mind is not. Perhaps we ought to use mindless as the term we mean instead of mindful. When I am full of my mind, I am empty of experience. Life feels so much more real when I am not there looking at it. Perhaps I need to re-think the idea of who this thing I call "I" really is. Perhaps this "I" still exists, albeit in a different form, when I am not locked in my head observing. Perhaps there's another place, other than my mind, where this "I" can reside, another form in which this "I" can be.

In considering the loss or shift in self that must occur, it is understandable that the self-judging voices intensify as you hover on the edge of flow. The interruptive voices get louder and stronger as your frightened mind fights for what it thinks is its last breath. How does it know for sure that it will return? The seemingly I-less existence made possible by your craft is thus a great threat to the I who begins the performance.

LOSING CONTROL

Entering into the zone means giving up control. Watching yourself from the outside feels safe and controllable while the zone (where you are part of and interchangeable with your experience) can seem unpredictable and scary. Have compassion for your frightened self. Consider the future it sees. By trying to maintain control, it *thinks* it is protecting you. Its limited vision however, prevents it from recognizing the infinite possibilities sacrificed in the name of that "control." Despite what your self-preserving mind may think, *you* are more than just your mind. In fact, your mind is not only *not* all there is to you, but on the court or stage, that mind may be a hindrance. By crossing the precipice into flow, you are demonstrating great courage, agreeing to take a chance, leaving the comfortable confines of your observing self. You are departing the safe zone and setting out on a journey across the protective distance that separates you from your experience. You cannot be both in your head and fully *in* your performance. As destinations, the two are incompatible. Have courage—where you are going is worth the trip.

12

RELISHING THE UNKNOWN

*There is nothing more exciting
than not knowing what's going to happen
while knowing that you're prepared for anything.*

K ara, a highly disciplined and accomplished show-
jumper came to me with the following complaint: her
training sessions were consistently superb but her
performances were not up to the same level of excellence.
While she was good in the show ring, she was certainly not
the great athlete her practice sessions showed she could be.
To her dismay and frustration, she was becoming known as a
rider who couldn't rise to the challenge of competition.
"What is there to do?" she desperately wanted to know.

In one of our initial meetings, I asked Kara how she
thought about her performance, the few minutes she would
spend in the ring actually competing. Amidst what sounded

like the very well-rehearsed answer of an athlete who had been the recipient of a lot of coaching and knew the "mentally tough" things to say, I detected one very telling statement. When considering her performance, she said that she hoped she would be able to "coast on her homework." While it could have passed for an "evolved" comment (as if she were simply going to allow her body to do its job), the word "coast" disturbed me. As we talked further, I discovered that my hunch was correct: the word was indeed indicative of the bigger problem. For Kara, the time in the ring was a kind of non-existent space. She worked as hard and was as prepared, physically, as any athlete I had ever treated. But for the few minutes of actual performance, she would stop paying attention to what was happening between her and her horse. In short, she became paralyzed.

Many of the performers I work with consider the actual time on stage as a time to simply survive. They dread the experience of not knowing what's going to happen. The fear of being in this unknown pervades every thought of their performance. When performers talk about their experience on stage they often become passive entities, saying things like "I hope it all goes well" or that "everything turns out OK." What is consistent is their conception of the event, namely, that *they* are no longer there to *make* that performance go well. They are not present within those unknown moments that occur inside "the ring" and thus can't be sure that they will adequately make use of their knowledge and skill. The element of unknown, in and of itself, is perceived as a dangerous force and something they cannot manage. In the face of this unknown, they agree to relinquish their own presence and skill, to lay down their sword before this beast that they envision. All that is left is to resign themselves to simply hoping for the best, trusting their homework to get them through. A recipe for greatness this is not. You must decide to stick around for the moments of not knowing. Do you want to reach your full potential? If so, your presence at all times is not only requested, it is required.

Your experience of performing is created by the thoughts you think. You can take control of those thoughts beginning right now. It is important to think about the "ring" as a place you *want* to be present, a time you look forward to, an opportunity. Easier said than done? Not if you shift your focus from imposing predictability to enjoying unpredictability!

Your performance is made up of a collection of unknown moments, moments you can't yet know or predict. How you perceive these moments before you live them, however, is something you *can* know and control. Instead of thinking of this unknown as your enemy or something to survive, what if you were to conceive of it as something exciting? What if you were to imagine it as an opportunity to be totally present, completely "in" your experience, completely involved, waiting and watching to see what unfolds before you. What if you were to relish this unknown time as an opportunity to exist on the freshest edge of your own life? Instead of trying to get through the experience, think of joining it, settling "in" to exactly the place in the performance where you actually are. Be there; invite your mind to enter this unknown in the same way that your body does each time it walks into "the ring." Re-think those spaces in the performance where, until now, you have felt lost and frightened. Perhaps you might be able to get excited about the potential that exists in those moments.

One thing is certain: with the unknown as your enemy, you will forever be trying to escape it, to close the gap. As a result, you will be inclined to rush your decisions, get ahead of yourself and try to make something happen before its time. When the unknown becomes a place that you can reside, the frenzy and impatience subsides. Without the frenzy, you can be present, loose and relaxed. These are the ingredients in the soup of peak performance.

TRUSTING YOUR BODY

Trusting the wisdom of your body is one of the most important lessons of a performer's career. Your *body's* knowledge is separate from that of your mind. Your body has a wealth of information and talent that exists in a completely different reservoir, one which cannot be controlled or even fully understood by your mind. P.C., a figure skater, put it this way "I now realize that my body actually exists as a physical entity and has indeed been there in all those training sessions, that it's not just my mind going through the drills. It's like I just got it that my body has an existence all its own, complete with its own form of memory and knowledge."

Consider what your body is doing for you at this very second without your telling it a thing. Your body knows *its* job. *Your* job, on the other hand, is to get out of the way and trust that body to do what it knows. Like a boss who refuses to delegate responsibility to those who are better at their jobs than he, your controlling mind costs you your optimal performance. *Humble your mind.* Greatness happens when you *let* your body do its job without trying to make it behave. Give this incredible being called your body *the chance* to show you what *it* can do. When you quiet your ego-centered mind, you allow your body to access *its own* pool of knowledge.

Finally, with you no longer in its way, your body can listen to its own wisdom. With you off its back, it's free to actually move.

BEING QUIET

The work goes on at home, in training. Figure it out there. Once you get to the performance, it's time to back off and *let* your physical wisdom take over. Often performers will report being surprised by how well they perform when exhausted or hung over from a late night of partying. This is not at all surprising; it is in just these instances that the thinking *you* is forced to get out of the way and let the physical and instinctive you take over. Your body is finally allowed to do its job as your mind is too tired to interrupt the process. Your body will take you to the top but only if you will trust and let it.

13

BECOMING REAL: SHEDDING THE IMPOSTOR

Right now is your real life.
It's not going to happen, it is happening.

∽

A client writes:

When will I learn to take myself seriously, to accept that I am not a would-be version of the person I am going to be? I am that person right now—this is my real life, my one existence. Am I pretending to be serious about my life or actually being serious? It seems that I have remained outside my life, postponing it, observing it as opposed to really living it. Am I playing the part of a real person/ professional or being it? I know that I must step into my own life, join my experience, get connected to me. Without this, everything I live feels make-believe—an arm's length away from me. Regardless of what I may feel, I am not a figment of my imagination, my life is not imaginary. One thing I do know is that I and it will expire as surely as those that I deem "real" in my mind. My imagined unrealness will not protect me from the passage of time nor death.

To understand what it is to become real, we must first examine what it is to feel unreal. Internal falseness creates the feeling of being a little kid who is playing at having a real life, living a life that has not yet and will never really begin. You are not legitimate in the same way that others are. No matter how much time and hard work you invest or how much you accomplish, you remain a fake, a pseudo-contender. When you feel unreal you are a fraud who is duping the world into thinking that you know something or are somebody. No matter how well you pretend, *you* know your knowledge and skills are unreliable, purely smoke and mirrors.

Feeling false causes you to distrust everything you know. Secretly you feel disconnected from your knowledge, as if it isn't you who owns or lives it. Any success you achieve is a fluke, something you got away with. It is difficult to internalize your success because, as far as you're concerned, it doesn't really exist. After all, if you are not real, everything you create is an illusion. Your achievements are transparent, meaningless, completely without weight or substance. No matter what this false you accomplishes, your *true* (unsuccessful, unreal) self knows better. Always in danger of being found out (for the fake that you are) you must be ever-conscious of covering up your falseness, pretending not to be the impostor that you are.

Becoming Real: Shedding the Imposter

If people knew better or I let myself look at my own success, we would all realize that none of it existed, including me. This being the case, I am lucky to get away with anything positive, best to just leave it be. If I point to it or let myself feel it, it will surely disappear. How can it disappear when it doesn't really exist? Perhaps it is not that it will become unreal since it already is that, but rather that I will be discovered and humiliated for the as-if winner that I am.

Feeling unreal can create a sense that you don't really exist, that someone could put his hand right through you because you are there only in ghost-like form. You don't feel as if your experiences become a part of you because, as far as you're concerned, there is no you for them to become a part of. You may be surprised each time you show up in a photograph or someone recognizes you from the past, any tangible evidence that suggests you exist. The idea that you had been there, or anywhere, that *you* actually took up space somewhere is baffling. In your own mind, you are a phantom.

Trusting your body to know what to do requires the belief that it was indeed *your* body participating in all those practice sessions.

A tennis player explains:

I'm still hazy on the fact that it was actually me out there in all those tournaments, or, for that matter, on the court each morning at five a.m. serving buckets of balls until my fingers bled. I know people tell me I was there and somewhere in me I remember it, but it doesn't feel like it was me. If it was, shouldn't it feel like a part of my life? If you asked me whether I knew anything about tennis, I would say yes and I suppose, mean it. But the truth is, deep down I don't really feel like I've ever swung a racquet in my life. It's no wonder that each time I walk onto the court to compete I am convinced this will be the time I have dreaded, the moment when my ignorance reveals itself, when it becomes clear that I have no experience whatsoever and am just a stark novice.

Another down-side to feeling unreal is that success merely raises you to the level of mediocrity, nothing more. Success gives you only the smallest degree of legitimacy—it translates to a minimal level of existence, albeit temporary. You are starting from such a place of falseness and make-believe that success is necessary just to put you on the map. Excitement would be ridiculous when success is just about getting to exist.

More from the tennis player:

Winning was simply something I had to do, the bare minimum I expected of myself. Anything less than clear victory amounted to complete nothingness, utter humiliation. Nothing less than perfection was permissible in the eyes of my internal judges. Success was the ticket to simply existing—it allowed me to break even, to not be a laughing stock. This system didn't leave much room for anything as decadent as joy, excitement or confidence.

ONLY THE BEST

When you feel like an impostor, there is tremendous pressure to do things in the *most* impressive of ways. In the desperate attempt to appear real, you must associate only

with the best coaches, players, artists and equipment—
whatever and whoever is available to make up for the
illegitimacy you actually feel. By attaching yourself to what
you perceive to be real, you have the chance to be seen as real
yourself—your important associations are a part of your
facade. As a bonus, your association with these legitimate
others can serve as pseudo-legitimacy for you. You *must* exist,
or why else would all these important people be around you?
Doesn't their associating with you and treating you as one of
their own make it so? Unfortunately, no degree of external
acceptance can create the internal validation you're so
desperately needing. The more impostor-like you feel, the
more symbols of importance you will be compelled to
accumulate in order to compensate for and hide your own
inadequacy. Anything that carries the faintest hint of
mediocrity or smallness will bring your own falseness to light
and is thus, your worst fear.

From a rider's journal:

*I wonder how I managed to go from never having
competed in a horse show to riding on the most
competitive National horse show circuit, all within a
period of months and without batting an eye. In my
mind, that's what was expected of top riders, and
after all, that's what I was. Within one year of owning
my very first horse, at a time when other riders would
have been competing at small, local shows, not me. I
wouldn't have been caught dead in any "backyard"
horse show, nor did I have any intention of riding on
any goofy college circuit, no matter how much fun it
might have been. No sir, I was commuting to Palm
Beach on my weekends, spending every dime I had to
compete against the best riders in the country (for*

which I was completely unprepared). It could have and should have been overwhelming, and yet, it wasn't even the smallest of big deals. If it had been a big deal or even just a tiny bit exciting, my cover would have been blown (both internally and externally). If I was indeed the real thing then this was nothing more than where I belonged. No one would accuse me of being some wide-eyed amateur. Excitement implied mediocrity. There was no appropriate time to be mediocre (or unprepared). It was straight to the top for me. Pretending to be a top rider allowed me to avoid the anxiety that would have been entirely unacceptable as well as entirely appropriate.

THE REAL DEAL

The first step in becoming real is shedding the notion that real winners are born and not made, that there is some inherent *special* quality that the "real" possess, a God-given difference between you and those who have this magical "it." In this childish system, winners must come out of the womb fully formed, without any need for development or learning.

A client explains:

In my way of thinking, winners arrive as winners and are never anything but winners. It was not permissible to have developed into the talented player I am today. Once the cat's out of the bag that I wasn't born this way but, embarrassingly, had to grow into my expertise, I again feel like an impostor, entirely illegitimate. In my system, being a winner is an inherent quality one either has or doesn't but not something one can grow into or earn. Clearly I don't have it or I would have been tapped on the shoulder long ago. The winner must arrive perfect, having done her developing and learning (if necessary at all), somewhere out of sight—in another lifetime, if possible.

Indeed there is an inherent difference between being real and unreal, it's called *work*. Ask yourself, if you were choosing a guide to take you rock climbing, would you want a leader who had gotten to the top by air-lift or one who had scaled the rock herself, discovering each of the paths and footholds on her own? True realness comes from covering the ground yourself. Gained ground cannot be lost; once you know it, you know it. Knowing it is what makes you real. It's the nitty-gritty, day-to-day, *un*-magical work that awards players with this winner's quality. The quality that you consider so magical, so God-given, is really no more than genuine knowledge and experience, evidence of having climbed the mountain.

To consider the possibility of my own hard work is to truly believe that I exist in my sport, that I am a real contender, a...dare I say it, winner. Cluing into all the hard work I've done reminds me that I am real, that I know my craft and that I have what it takes. Reminding myself of this fact makes me feel very special—not because I was born special, but because I have had the courage and fortitude to become an expert at something, because I am somebody who has put in the effort that winning demands. It sounds so unglamourous (put that way), but it is as exciting a thought as I have ever known.

IT DOES MATTER

In order to become real you must first give up the facade that nothing matters and/or that nothing about you should be taken seriously. What would happen if you were to admit to yourself (and others) that what you are doing *is* important to you, that what happens to you does matter? What if you allowed yourself to express your real passion? Would that be dangerous? Would you be at risk for failure or humiliation? Would you look silly? If so, to whom? What would it be like for you to care about something, to take something seriously, to, dare I say it, take yourself seriously?

FEELINGS

In distinguishing between yourself and the "real" players, do you assume that "real players" have no need for feelings, never get nervous, never have doubts and fears? Nerves, after all, would imply that their success meant something to them, that it was more than just something they got done between brushing their teeth and putting on their shoes. It would mean that it was a real and difficult event for which they worked very hard. Real players wouldn't get excited either; excitement would imply that their success was somehow a big deal (the greatest of all sins). This kind of thinking creates a state of deadness in which nothing at all is deemed worthy of your emotion and thus you're not allowed to live any of it fully or authentically.

More from my client:

I can never express any happiness when I win, that would be amateurish. I should be winning after all. For me, displaying excitement translates to admitting that I didn't expect to win; there should be nothing exciting about doing the expected. Emotion advertises my anticipation of lesser things, that my "norm" is losing. So too, I can never get nervous even before the biggest national competitions. None of it, none of me is acceptable. Real riders don't get stressed. For them, nerves are not a problem. What do they have to be nervous about? They know they can count on themselves to ride brilliantly. I conduct myself like a paper cut-out which only adds to the unreality of my experience.

I can remember the first time I admitted to my trainer that I was nervous before walking in the ring. Something actually made it through the armor. The result was that I had said it out loud—this mattered to me—it was out there for whatever anyone wanted to do with it. My worst fears were out there to be tested. It was not so much progress that made this possible as overwhelming anxiety that could no longer be contained. I actually feared fainting right there on the horse. I had to warn my trainer. But something unexpected happened as a result. Coming clean with my fear proved entirely liberating and actually caused the anxiety to lift. Suddenly I was there, I was real, I existed. It was OK that I had feelings, that I was human. I felt none of the embarrassment I had for so many years expected the admission of emotion to cause me.

Why bother doing it if I can't feel it? To remove the emotion and be perpetually "blasé," is to effectively vacuum the passion from the very thing I feel most passionate about. Curious, why would I choose to do that? Passion is the reason to bother living, the rest of *it is just tasteless filling like the inside of a Twinkie without the sugar. Why would I deny myself the experience of "meaning" in my life—ironically—not the activity itself, but the meaning derived from it. Is it me who purposefully seeks to make my own life meaningless?*

Here's the truth: "real players" get nervous, "real players" get excited. "Real players" are, in fact, just people despite what you may think. Performing at any level is nerve-wracking. It is exciting to succeed no matter how often or rarely it happens. In order to reach the top, you've not only got to want it, you've got to admit to yourself and others that you want it. The pure act of expressing your feelings changes you; it makes you feel more connected to your craft and as a result, more real. Feelings put you there, they allow you to be *present* in the experience. Without the feeling, nothing about your passion can sink in—not the joy, dedication, knowledge, commitment, involvement, relationships, identity, none of it. You are shut out of your own life.

A rider recounts an important realization:

I overheard two big time riders talking about their anxiety, trading horror stories about the possible outcomes of the day's course. It was so shocking to me; there they were having a laugh at their own nerves.

There it was: the truth. Real riders—top riders—all of us scared. It was only me who was embarrassed by my emotions. Standing there at the in-gate of this grueling course was indeed a terrifying experience. Only I assumed that being real meant having no feelings, existing in a dead zone where nothing affects you. It was me who was the untouchable, unreal, caricature of a rider. Where did all those feelings over all those years actually go? I have been so cruel to myself, putting away all that fear to say nothing of my passion and excitement. How did I stuff it all away? It is amazing even to me that I was able to silence such intense emotions, further proof for how powerful was my need to hide my true feelings, particularly those fears and desires that were strongest. How terribly sad, to be so afraid and yet have nowhere to turn, for when I turned inside I found only embarrassment, condemnation and loathing for my own terror. There was no place of support, and thus, I was forced to anesthetize my feelings and function in a numb silence. Where did this leave me? How could I expect myself to feel free and able to access my potential in this sort of prison? How rejected and alone I have left myself, with literally nowhere to go but away from my feelings and me.

NEEDS AND RIGHTS

Another aspect of becoming real involves learning to respect and defend our own needs and rights. We must learn to believe that we are entitled to make demands and be treated with respect. Becoming real includes knowing that what we want matters because we matter. We are not required to tolerate whatever treatment we receive. Each of us is a real person with feelings and needs! We must learn to defend ourselves as we would a good friend, not because we know we're *supposed* to, but because we genuinely believe that we deserve respect and a certain quality of treatment. The pure act of standing up for ourself can, in and of itself, encourage the process of becoming real.

A rider explains:

I can remember the day I made my first real demand in my sport. I was scheduled to have a 10 a.m. lesson on the grounds of a horse show an hour's drive from my home. It was 10 a.m. and my trainer had yet to arrive. Ten-thirty brought his van just pulling into the stabling area. My instinct, tragically, was to disappear, to not be standing there as the first thing he saw when he arrived. My worst fear—to be a bother, to stand out, to be a nuisance, to have needs.

I imagined his thoughts, "What a drag. Now I have to deal with her, this would-be athlete." Since I was just a joke, who on earth was I to be irritated by this kind of treatment? "I pay my bills," I whispered to myself, trying to generate some conviction, some belief that I deserved better. How tragic, that paying my bills was all I could think of to stimulate a feeling of legitimacy.

Truth is, I didn't believe I was legitimate; I was trying to win the case in my own head. I was discounting, of course, that I was one of the most successful riders on the circuit at the time. None of that (or me) seemed real in that moment. And so I did what I always do, make myself scarce, come back later when I wouldn't be in the way. When I arrived later, my own feelings appropriately suppressed, I would pretend to be late myself, ever-careful to avoid making anyone else uncomfortable or responsible for his or her abuse of me. I popped in a few minutes later to find my groom leisurely attending to the business of setting up our stalls while not yet preparing my horse to be ridden. "I have somewhere to be at 1:00" I said without any irritation in my voice. In the end, I began my lesson at 11:30, an hour and a half late, no apologies made. As I was preparing to leave the grounds, I asked an assistant to "do me a favor" and take a piece of equipment back to the barn area. She informed me that she "wasn't sure (she) could remember to do that." In retrospect, small words for the grand change they were to inspire in my life.

Driving home, now late for my own appointment, I snapped. Raging, I pulled into a gas station and called my trainer. Sternly, I informed him of how he had inconvenienced me, of how his assistant had spoken to me. I said the word "me" with new-found power and conviction, genuine indignation. This "me" was one of his top riders, one of his biggest sources of reputation and income. I just got it—I did more than just pay my bills. In an instant, the separation between what my mind told me I deserved and what I felt I deserved had vanished. I was, of course, not just angry about this particular episode, but responding to a lifetime of mistreatment, all condoned and welcomed by me. I had asked for nothing, expected nothing and in return, gotten nothing. It was me who had trained people how to treat or rather, mistreat me. I didn't respect my own presence so how could they be expected to?

The real anger was for myself, not my trainer. I had not honored my own needs, living my life according to what others wanted and needed, what I imagined they expected. It is me who set up a system in which even common courtesy did not apply to me, me who created the monster at whose hands I now suffered. Since that day, it is not an exaggeration to say that everything has changed. My external world has shifted as a result of the change in my internal world. From the moment I began exposing my own needs, I understood what it meant to feel real and thus deserving. I have since been able to ask for and get what I want. Amazingly, I am no longer surprised or uncomfortable when I get it. I am surprised and bothered when I don't! When you take yourself seriously, you are indeed taken seriously by others. Even if I weren't this successful or talented, I would still deserve to be treated with respect, because I, as a person, matter. Sometimes I wonder if all my striving and achieving has been an effort to generate this feeling of self-worth. Did I think that if I were just successful enough, important enough, I would then be of value to myself and others? If I proved myself as worthy, would I no longer need to convince myself that I was worthy of defending? Unfortunately, there is no such thing as enough. No amount of accomplishment could create this feeling of self-respect. My successes just piled up on top of a worthless me. The me who has rights is the original me, the one underneath all the glory, the core me.

The message: make demands and stand up for yourself even before you feel you have that right. (Fake it before you can make it.) You cannot live a real life without expressing and acknowledging your own needs; although it may feel like it some times, you are in fact not a cartoon cut-out. When you start making your needs known, as uncomfortable as it may feel, everything around and inside you will begin to shift. It is then that your real life can begin.

SACRIFICE

More from this same rider:

Were I to take my sacrifices seriously, I would then have to admit to myself how much I care about what happens and how important this craft really is to me. This too would mean demanding a seriousness from those with whom I interact. It would mean taking responsibility for the enormous financial, emotional, spiritual, time and life investment I am making. I have spent my entire life pretending to take myself and my passion seriously. Internally, it has always felt like a vacuum. None of my hard work or sacrifice was real to me. My experience was taking place only externally. Even my own desire was something I could put my hand through. I take up space purely as a result of those around me; the reflection from my environment lands on me, creating the illusion that I am there.

Do you ever stop to honor and acknowledge all that you are *giving up* for your passion? Becoming "real" involves taking responsibility for how you choose to live. Take a good hard look at what you are choosing to have and not have in your life. Take the blinders off. Stop pretending that your life is just happening to you. Become aware of and assume an *active* role in your own life decision making. You are making choices whether you take responsibility for them or not. Look at what you are actually doing; acknowledge what you want and what you are giving up for it.

When you feel like an impostor, your sacrifice and hard work is either discounted or destroyed. "If you are giving up so much, why aren't you the real thing?" "Who are you to say that it's hard!" Remember the desire and willingness to make sacrifices for something is not only a gift but something to be proud of, something that takes great courage. It is not only where that sacrifice *gets* you, your sacrifice is important in and of itself. Regardless of whether you become a "star," there is incredible honor in purely working hard at something. Take credit for that hard work. Doing anything well requires great sacrifice. You make sacrifices because what you are doing is important to you. You *want* it and wanting is a good thing, an important admission. As long as you deny your own sacrifice, you will not be able to own your passion nor feel deserving of its rewards.

Make a list of what you are giving up—time, money, other interests, vacations, friends, food and much more. Refrain from chastising yourself as you do this, just look at what shows up. These sacrifices are not a figment of your imagination; they are very real. Acknowledging (and respecting) the sacrifices you are making helps create a connection between you and your experience; it makes you feel more real. In addition, when you are in touch with your own hard work, success becomes something *you* feel you deserve as opposed to an imaginary event to which you are unconnected. The more you feel you deserve success, the more probable your success becomes.

CREATING A YOU

Feeling unreal is a result of not being connected to yourself or your life. This happens when big parts of you are put to sleep or ignored. By learning to acknowledge all the various aspects of yourself—feelings, needs, rights, fears, sacrifice, hard work, desire, etc., you are literally recognizing a *you*. You are the combination of all of these ingredients. Unless you can feel these ingredients, there can be no you. With each ingredient that you shortchange or ignore, a little piece of your experience is lost, a part of you anesthetized. The result is that *you* (and your life) become less real and more like an illusion.

THE HARDEST WORDS OF ALL: I DON'T KNOW

Keep in mind, becoming real is based on developing real knowledge. Real knowledge can only occur when you are willing to say "I don't know," when your goal shifts from trying to *appear* knowledgeable to actually wanting to *be* so. You must want to *be* an expert as opposed to wanting to *look* like one. When you have the courage to admit your ignorance and start asking questions, you will then start establishing your own base of knowledge and realness. For Kirsten, a rider who had been around horses her entire life, every show was a test to see if she could successfully hide her ignorance. She was a leading competitor, considered by her peers to know everything there was to know about horses. Underneath the facade, however, she felt utterly inept when it came to caring for her animals. Indeed, she was quite helpless despite all of the experience she had gained in her sport. No matter how much time she spent doing it, no matter how much success she earned, she remained an impostor, someone who was pretending to know about horses. The truth was, she did lack basic skills when it came to caring for the animals. Knowing that she *should* know more than she did, she was humiliated by her ignorance and further compelled to fake an expertise she didn't own. It was too late for questions. And yet, when she thought back to the beginning of her career, it seemed that it had always been too late for questions. Questions meant she didn't know everything. Why didn't she know everything? Real professionals surely knew everything. Not having learned it was no excuse for not knowing it. Learning was for average folks; questions were for amateurs, not her!

"And now, with all of my experience, I really *should* know it all, now it really *is* too late for ignorance," she bemoaned, feeling frustrated and trapped. Embarrassed, Kirsten confessed, "When I have to bandage horses legs, I feel like I have to fake it, like I never really learned and still don't know how to. I'm always sure I'm going to cripple the animal. It's pathetic."

Kirsten was convinced that her peers would be dumbfounded by how little she really knew. Her lack of knowledge served as more evidence that she didn't belong in her sport, that she wasn't one of the real players. She didn't know anything, so how could she be real? Real players would have the weight and substance of one who is filled with knowledge.

For Kirsten, feeling illegitimate had more to do with her relationship with her family than not knowing how to bandage horses' legs. My work with Kirsten was focused on helping her shift her self-image from one of a child who was defined by her family's judgments to that of an adult capable of making her own life choices. Gradually, Kirsten learned to respect her own judgment when it came to her life, to see her existence as belonging to her and not her family. As a result, she was better able to honor *her* choice to be a rider. The act of honoring her choice, believing that she was capable and responsible for deciding how to live her own life, thus contributed to her feeling more real and valid in the role she chose. She could finally let herself *be* a rider (in her own eyes) and inhabit her identity as such. By honoring her own choice, she became real in her own mind. Her need to ask questions, subsequently, became less humiliating. Knowing everything ceased to be a requirement for legitimacy as she felt more internally legitimate. For the first time, she actually wanted to know the answers instead of simply needing to *seem* as if she knew them. Not needing to know everything thus opened the door to her being able to know something.

SHATTERING THE MYTH

You will have arrived at real when you can look at the top players shining in the spotlight and realize that there is no difference between you and them, when you can realize how possible and available the winner's circle has *always* been to you, when you give up the inherent disparity between you and these mythical winners. You can then imagine yourself winning, existing in what used to be "their" world, but which is now "yours" as well. The winner's world belongs to those who are courageous enough to inhabit it, willing enough to work for it and committed enough to make it theirs. It is at this stage that the halo fades from around the winner's circle and leaves it there to exist like any other round patch of earth on which you too can stand.

Our rider continues:

I can remember with complete vividness the first awards presentation I ever witnessed. Oh, I had watched hundreds before but this one was different. It was a perfect spring afternoon, the sun was sparkling, which made the purple flowers around the ring glow. As always, the division champion rode into the ring alone and while still mounted was presented with her ribbon and trophy. The winning rider on this day was a fresh-looking blond girl, smiling as she leaned her head down from her huge bay thoroughbred to accept the medal around her neck. The steward waved the ribbon to encourage her horse's ears to prick forward for the photograph. The scene was the same as always, and yet as I sat there looking on, I became intensely aware of my own presence and where I was physically seated in relation to the winner's circle. It felt as if the girl and her horse were right under my nose even though they were a good twenty feet away. Also, I became aware of the fact that I was not watching a movie, not witnessing the event from far, far away as it usually seemed.

I had the distinct sensation that the fog through which I normally viewed these presentations had dispersed. I was able to notice specifics in the picture: the fact that the girl's stirrup leather needed re-stitching, the wet spot on her jacket where her horse had drooled, the whiteness of her teeth when she smiled, the fly on her horse's hind end and much, much more.

Becoming Real: Shedding the Imposter

It felt like someone had adjusted the focus knob behind my eyes. As the photographer snapped the girl's picture, I found myself thinking intently about her trip around the course and specifically how skillfully she had ridden one particular corner. As I watched this award ceremony, the performance itself was not a forgotten, unrelated event as it usually was. The award around her neck, for the first time, was connected to that ride. Suddenly, this young girl with perfect attire, sparkling white teeth and a beautiful face to match her beautiful horse, was nothing more and nothing less than a talented rider. She was no longer a magical princess in a fairly tale, but a rider who, on this particular day, had brilliantly negotiated the course-at-hand.

Until that moment, everything in my sport (including my own involvement), had felt like a scene in a movie, something I was watching but not a part of. And now, finally, the director had yelled "cut." The star pulled off her wig, the pink-tinted lights went dark, the haze-making machines cut off, the caterer came in to re-stock the bagels and there it was. What was left was only the revealing light of the overhead sun. Reality. That's all it ever was. A young girl who had trained hard and successfully ridden today's course.

14

INHABITING YOUR LIFE

Take up residence in your own life.
Abandon everything but never yourself.

∽

News flash: this place called *there* to which you so desperately want to arrive, it doesn't exist. You can't be *there*. Once you get *there*, it instantly becomes *here*. In truth, the only place you can be is *here*.

WHOSE LIFE IS IT ANYWAY?

What would it mean for you to enter your own life? What would it mean to stop running from right now and the you who is living it? Can you turn your attention to the life you are living at this moment? Entering your own life means choosing to stop dismissing *here* simply because it is where *you* are, to stop rejecting and ignoring your own life in the hopes of entering some other life that isn't yours, to stop seeing *there* as perpetually better because it is where you are *not*.

The first step in entering your own life is accepting that this *is* your life. Sounds like an obvious statement, right? The truth is, few people take the meaning of this statement to heart. You probably have some vague notion of what your *real* life will be. Most likely, it is going to begin at some point in the future when you become a success or maybe when you get married, buy a house, have kids or whatever *there* is for you. But certainly this right now, this training session, this problem you are grappling with today, this competition, this performance—these are merely obstacles on the way to your real life, not the real life itself. The truth is, no *now* is going to feel more like your real life than this one. Inhabiting your life means accepting this now as the one that matters. This life that you woke up to today is the one that counts.

Regardless of how old you are, the process is the same: internally accepting that your life belongs only to you, that your existence is truly in your own care. It is you who must take your own life seriously, and consequently, take seriously the daily decisions you make that shape that life.

RIGHT NOW

What will make today's life feel real is in fact a lot simpler than what you may imagine. The answer lies in your attention. Consider what it would mean to begin living the life you are in today—this morning's practice session, today's conversation with a friend, this morning's walk in the park, these words you are reading, all these small "unimportant" events. Life is nothing more than the sum of moments you are living, a necklace strung with your day-to-day experiences. That's it.

Within that simple *it* however, lies the infinite possibility that is a real life. It's both much less and much more magical than you imagine. Taking this truth to heart can be terrifying; if this really is your life, then why haven't you been paying attention to it? If this moment really is *it*, then this moment really matters. Given that it matters, should you be inhabiting it differently? Recognizing the immediacy of your life generates enormous possibility as well as responsibility. Frightening though it may be, to accept the reality of your life is to accept the unfathomable meaning of (and in) right now. To do this is to open the door to a life worth living.

IF NOT NOW, WHEN?

Nancy-Jo, a figure skater, came into my office ecstatic. She announced that she had made a major decision. Starting on that day, she was *only* going to be performing in the costumes she adored, the ones she really wanted to wear. "Why am I always skating in outfits I hate? Why is it *still* not the right time for me to look great on the ice? Why is my real skating career always being postponed—always scheduled for sometime in the future?

For over 10 years, Nancy-Jo had refused to spend her money on "the good stuff" because this, after all, wasn't her *real* skating career. She had always thought she would buy the right clothes when she got "there." Even though she was competing and training quite seriously, the present had never been infused with any real urgency or value. How could she take herself seriously *now*? Everything was on hold until "later" when she would be a "real" skater. Unfortunately, time continued to pass despite her illusions of a "life on hold." Seasons came and went, junior divisions became senior, and Nancy-Jo was still skating in her crummy attire, hating the way she looked and being overlooked by the judges because of her amateur-like costumes. In essence, postponing her "real" career was preventing her "real" career. Suddenly, on this particular day, she had decided that it was time to treat this performance, this outfit, these sequins, this now, this life, this *her*, as the real thing. It was time to start treating right now as all there was, time to start making herself happy, to start living this moment as if it counted. As she put it, "The simple fact that I am going to be skating onto the ice in this costume tonight is reason enough for it to be everything I want. If not tonight, when *will* it be time for me to look the part? I have to make it now."

YOUR EPITAPH

Imagine that you are listening to someone describe your life after it's over. Are you surprised by what you hear? Does it sound like a life you would have wanted to live? Have you the urge to interrupt with a "Yes, that may have been how I lived my life, but that wasn't really *my life*." Newsflash: *how you live your life is your life*. The choices you make each day, the individual moments you live, this is all there is. Your choices must not sound disconnected to who you "really" are. If you're lucky, you get about eighty years on this planet, eighty years of their being a *you*. Instead of living your life in a constant state of distraction, of always being somewhere but not here, what if you were to start paying attention to the life that's in front of you right now, to start treating today's choices and experiences as if they matter? What then?

A client writes on the subject of now:

My life has been happening for 30 years. Is this really it? When I die, won't it all be a big joke? Surely someone will open my coffin and say "Come on out, that wasn't your real life, now go and live the one that really counts." Wrong. As I ride better and better, I realize that today, this horse show, this course, these jumps, this is it. This is all there is. Today my horse may jump well or he may not. He may get caught in the mud or knock a rail. But above all else, I must enjoy the process because the process is all there is, the process is as real as it gets, the process is my life.

I used to think that I would be complete once I got to where I was going; once I became a winner I would have a real life and my would-be life would suddenly switch from pause to play. I now see that the result, winning, has nothing to do with feeling real. Not only that, but the best way to start winning is to stop making it about winning. The joy must come from doing the thing itself and not from what it may or may not bring as a result. My goals must lay within the process.

Now that I'm at the top, the place from which everything was supposed to look and feel different, the magical spot where it was all supposed to change, I can see the reality. It's still just about this course, this problem, this challenge of today. Winner or not, it's still just me out there wrestling with the moment. Inhabiting my life is about inhabiting each moment, being fully here in whatever experience I am in. Ironically, being "here" can create its own kind of pressure. Now that this moment matters, it is imperative that I take it seriously, make something out of it, do something with it. I have to pay attention to my own choices. I can't take my own life for granted any longer. I can now create the life I want because I am finally inside it. This is exciting.

Most folks spend their entire lives looking for something that they really want to do. Few people have something in their life for which they are willing to make real sacrifices, something they *want* to do when they get up in the morning. If you have been blessed (and it is indeed nothing less than a blessing) to feel true passion, treat your passion as the unbelievable gift that it is. Because it is a blessing does not mean that it comes without problems. It does mean however, that you want to solve these problems, that you know you *must* solve these problems. This is precisely what makes it a gift. There is nothing more serious or important than the choice of how to spend the individual moments of your life, this moment right now included. Treat this choice with the seriousness it deserves. If you have been blessed with something you *want* to do with your time, don't waste it by doubting your choice, honor it by living it.

Judging your particular passion as unworthy or silly is another way to resist entering your life. To question and invalidate your "choice of passion" (as if there is a choice) is to decide that you are not capable of choosing how to live your own life. It is a way of remaining child-like, refusing to take responsibility for your own choices. Who is more qualified than you to choose how you should live your life? Isn't it time to start paying attention to your own opinion, honoring your own decisions? Your choices are valid precisely because you choose them. Your choices reflect who *you* are; they need not be related to anyone but you. It is hard enough to succeed when you believe in what you are doing. When you add the extra obstacle of doubting the validity of your efforts, it becomes impossible.

Passion is passion. There is no passion inherently more worthy than another. What is important is not the activity itself, but how you as the participant feel about it. For competitors who reach the top, their own presence and interest, the fact that *they* want to be there is precisely what awards the activity with meaning. Some folks like to spin cars around a track, some collect old furniture. For others, thinking up words that rhyme or tapping a little ball into a hole in the ground is the best way to spend a life. The specific choice is irrelevant, what matters is that it is your choice, it is *you*. When you reject your passion, you reject your self. Your time belongs to you and no one else. These are your moments on this earth. How do *you* want to spend your moments? This is the only important question. However you answer it, take your choice to heart. The simple fact that it is *your* choice makes it valid.

ANYONE BUT YOU

Years ago when Robin lived in Virginia, there was a famous actress who rode with the same trainer as she did. The actress, who was just an intermediate rider, frequently complimented Robin on her riding skill, confessing her admiration and envy for Robin's talent. Often, the woman would come to watch Robin practice in the hopes of learning to ride more like her. Within this relationship, Robin was the defined star despite the actress being a real "movie star." In such moments when the "movie star" would express her admiration, Robin would swell with pride for her sport and herself. The words (coming from someone who mattered) made Robin important. Suddenly her sport was the most fascinating and worthy pursuit, not to mention an honorable passion to which to dedicate her own life. Being an expert rider made her special, but only when her "star" was around. The approval of someone whom she deemed important or worthy, whose opinion "meant" something, served to define her own feelings about herself. To Robin, the actress was not only famous, but "real," "adult" and "recognized," thus qualifying *her* to determine the validity of Robin's choices.

Perpetually searching for meaning in other people, places, labels, possessions, etc., is a way of abandoning yourself. Looking outside yourself for people and things that will make you matter only confirms the feeling that being with yourself is being nowhere. As a result, meaning is something that you can only get next to but never own or inhabit. You must become a destination worthy of inhabiting before anything else can have meaning. Until *you* matter, nothing *you* do matters.

There is great sadness in considering how often and much you abandon and ignore yourself, discounting your own feelings and opinions as you search for anything that will save you from being with the nothingness that you envision as *you*. Ask yourself, how do *you* feel being rejected and abandoned every day? How is this *self* (you) supposed to function when it knows that its existence, its value, is made possible only by the presence of external sources? Breaking free from the pack is about developing a sense of self that is separate from the momentary cheers or jeers of the crowd. There must be something internal, some private sense of OK-ness to which you can return when the cheering temporarily subsides, a self-generated belief in yourself that sustains itself regardless of the circumstance of the moment.

Have you ever had an opinion about yourself that was not based on someone else's? If not, make a decision right now to change this. Get in touch with the you who is out there training, working hard, wanting this success so intensely. This is *your* you. This is the you who is there regardless of whether you were brilliant today or had an off-day. Work on creating a bank of feeling, knowledge and faith in yourself that can serve as your private vault of confidence and compassion, one for which only you have the key. In those moments of imperfection, ask yourself, what *you* exists separate from today's foible? What about you remains worthy and legitimate? What about you is not destroyed by this moment's imperfection? Your own vision of you will become your safe harbor, your place of greatest strength. You are what *you* think of you and *not*, as you may have believed, the creation of others' opinions.

15

PRACTICAL
TECHNIQUES

~

KNOW THYSELF/CONTROL THE CONTROLLABLE

Surprisingly, even at the top, many performers under-estimate the power of planning. They make the mistake of playing their performance "by ear," leaving it in the hands of fate, hoping the conditions will favor them. No plan is a bad plan! You cannot guarantee a great performance, but you absolutely can guarantee that you have the best *chance* for a great performance. Performance is filled with the unknown and uncontrollable. As a result, it is especially important to know and control those factors that you can. Study yourself. Figure out every intimate detail of what works for you as a performer and what doesn't. Make a list of each of the concrete factors that contributes to your best per-formance. The better you know yourself as a performer (and abide by this knowledge), the better your odds of creating a peak performance. Keep in mind, getting to know yourself and writing down the results of your research takes work. It is always easier to "coast," to simply hope for the best, assuming that what works for you will be different with each performance. Each performance will be different, yes, but there are things about *you* that will always be true. Know these things. You will never create greatness by "coasting." Greatness is a result of one thing: hard work.

Here is a bare bones list of what you should know about yourself:

1. Who you should spend your time with on the day of, day before and during the week leading up to your performance.

2. Who you should invite to your performance.

3. How you should spend your time before your performance (relaxing, exercising, talking on the phone, being quiet, listening to music, practicing your performance, watching a movie, etc.).

4. How early to arrive at your performance site.

5. Whether to watch the performances (or matches) that precede yours.

6. How much sleep to get (or at the very least, what time to get in bed) the night before, and entire week before, your performance.

7. How much to "train" on the day of, day before and entire week before your performance.

8. What to eat on the day of, day before and entire week before your performance.

9. How much exercise to do on the day of, day before and entire week before your performance.

10. How (and with whom) you should travel to your performance (car, walk, train, bus, with a friend, a coach, a spouse, alone, etc.).

11. What you should listen to (music, talk, etc.) on route to, and prior to, your performance.

12. When to make use of your sensorization and breathing techniques; when (and if) to be alone in order to "center" yourself.

Fill in your own...

13.

14.

15.

16.

SENSORIZATION (of peak performance)

I use the term sensorization and not visualization for a reason. For many years, everything I read and everyone I talked to told me that visualization was the answer and that I had to learn to use my mind as a screen. If I couldn't *see* myself riding successfully in my mind, I would never ride successfully in the show ring. It sounded believable, certainly everybody agreed, and so I did what I was told. I tried like mad to visually imagine myself as successful, to create a visual image of my positive performances. The fact that this process was extraordinarily difficult for me, that the images did not come naturally, this I could have lived with. I was not afraid of hard work. What disturbed me however, was that these visual images seemed to have no impact on my performances. And worse, instead of feeling more confident, I was left feeling more frustrated and even more insecure. In my effort to become more successful and confident, I had determined only that my insecurity was justified: I was a visualization failure. My mind's eye was blind.

So what was my problem? Why did these visualization techniques that help so many performers simply not work for me? Was I really unable to create something that everyone else could create? Had I not bought the right book, found the right image, unveiled the right screen? If I couldn't see it, was I doomed to never be able to do it? The answer turned out to be quite simple (and relieving) although it took a long time (and a lot of frustration) to discover. Ironically, the way I did finally stumble upon it was through a simple game with a friend, nothing at all to do with my sport.

I was taking a walk with two friends on a freezing New York afternoon when one of them decided that in order to stay warm, we should imagine that we were at the beach. An unspectacular exercise, or so I thought. After a few minutes of walking quietly and experiencing our own imaginary beaches, we began sharing our mental journeys. What I heard changed my entire training style and consequently, my career. Kelly was first to speak. She marveled at the image of the sun going down at dusk, the blue of the sky, the aquamarine water, the way the sun reflected off the crisp white sand. Jane spoke of the crashing sound of the waves, the hum of a bird over the water, the fluffy white clouds passing effortlessly throughout the electric blue horizon. For me, it was all about the warmth of the sand between my toes, the refreshing wash of the water over my body, the feel of the cool air hitting my body as I came out of the water. I spoke of lying down on the warm towel as the sun melted the chill out of my bones, the lightness of the breeze as it brushed against my face, the feel of the cool iced tea against my throat. Suddenly I got it. I don't think visually, I don't think by way of hearing, I feel things! Put in fancy terms, I think kinesthetically! No wonder the years of trying to *see* things wasn't working, it wasn't who I am or how I think. Find out how you think before you choose a sensory technique to use in your training. If you're a "feeler" like me and spend all your time trying to "see" your best performances, you will be wasting your time; your images won't resonate because they're not in your language!

Play this same game with yourself (you may have to use a different setting) and notice how you describe the experience, whether you use mostly visual, sound, or feeling cues. Most people will use a combination of the three, but there is almost always a style that dominates.

So now that I know I'm kinesthetic, all of my imagining is done in terms of feeling. What did my body *feel* like during that peak performance? What was the sensation in my hands, legs, arms, etc.? What was the *feeling* in my belly when I was relaxed? How and where do I experience the effortlessness that typifies a brilliant course? What will my horse's stride *feel* like as I ride the turns of the course? What will the correct pace *feel* like as I approach the jumps? I don't attempt to see anything, but rather to lock in (and into) the *feelings* that accompany and define these positive and successful experiences. Because I am now communicating in the internal language of my body and mind, the exercises stick, my body stores the imaginary practice in its memory, and thus can make use of it in reality. From here forward, rather than repeat "visualize, hear, or feel" with each exercise, I will use the term "sensorize" to refer to the imagining process itself. Depending on your personal language, translate the exercises accordingly. A whisper in your native tongue does wonders; a shout that's not understood goes unheard. More people give up on this process NOT because they have a sluggish imagination (as they assume), but because they never clue into their own experiential style. If you've been communicating in the wrong language (as I was), you're in for a real treat. Fasten your seat belt—things are about to change!

SENSORIZE, SENSORIZE, SENSORIZE.

Sensorization equals opportunity. Sensorization offers you the chance to practice your performance whenever and wherever you are. Every second of every day you have access to a perfect practice field; your field is never closed and requires no travel time to get there. That field is your mind. Take advantage of the unlimited opportunity your imaginary stage offers. Communicating effectively with your body requires more than just *telling* it how you want it to perform. It is about learning to *sense* (see, feel and/or hear) yourself performing correctly. There are infinite uses for sensorization, but here are a few to incorporate into your daily training.

THE PEAK PERFORMANCE

Create a sense (image or feeling) of your best performance ever. Choose a performance when everything seemed easy, when you somehow "knew" that things were going to go your way, when your body moved exactly as it should. In other words, a time when you were "in the zone." Let your body *sense* this performance, don't *tell* yourself what you were doing right, see and/or feel it in your mind and body. Experience the physical feelings you had on that day, the looseness and comfort of your body. Let yourself re-enter this state of focused relaxation, settle into that confident place inside yourself.

Take a few minutes *every day* to run yourself through this performance, to literally imagine yourself playing that game, performing that piece. Put yourself back into the body and mind of that performance. Cement this memory into your consciousness. Become so familiar with the feelings and sensations associated with your peak performance that the mere thought of it triggers your body and mind to return to that state of confidence. Reliving your peak performance in your imagination, you invite your body and mind to re-enter the place where it was on that "perfect" day.

Create a sense of the events leading up to that performance. What were you thinking about? Who did you talk to right before walking onto the court/stage? Who did you spend time with on that day? How did you feel as you were waiting to begin? Which of your friends or family, if any, were there to watch you? How had you warmed up that day? How much had you slept the night before? What had you eaten on that day? What was your training schedule for that week? Know everything there is to know about your peak performance. Rehearse it in your mind (and body) over and over again, from start to finish. Know it so well that you can take yourself back there (and into that state) whenever you choose. Use the sense to generate that winning feeling just before you perform.

REACTION REHEARSAL

Most of you are probably already familiar with the peak performance rehearsal. Few of you, however, may be aware of or take full advantage of the opportunity your mind offers for rehearsing difficulty. You must use your mind to practice not only the experience of everything going right, but everything that could go wrong as well. Use your sensorizations to practice working through any and every problem that could arise on the field or stage.

Right now, the greatest challenge you face when a problem occurs is not the problem itself, but the fear (and surprise) that it generates. The problem is unknown (and thus frightening). This must change. Spend a few minutes every day sensing (seeing, feeling, hearing) a specific problem that might occur on the field. Run through it from start to finish. How will you deal with it? What will you do to adjust to the new situation? Sense yourself adjusting, rehearse your successful handling of the problem. Sensorization is under-used in its ability to *prepare* you for the unknown. Why create problems when they happen enough without your help? You create them in order to practice your reactions to them, in order to prepare your response. Sensing your reactions helps you turn an unknown and frightening event into one that is known and more predictable. Use your senses to be *ready* for the inevitable. Shying away from difficult situations leaves you simply *hoping* for the best, *hoping* that this game brings no such difficulty. Hoping for the best is not a game plan, it is being unprepared. Are you comfortable leaving your fate in the hands of hope or do you want to create it? Why not deal with these situations on your private practice stage, rehearse your responses where you have nothing to lose. Use the opportunity of sensorization to train yourself how to react, in both body and mind. Why not walk onto the field *prepared* for anything that could and will happen?

TODAY'S TASK

Before you begin competing, sense the specific performance you are going to deliver *today*. Include as many specifics as you can (audience, banners, weather conditions, colors, smells, etc.) Sense yourself playing today's notes, dancing today's steps, jumping today's course, diving into today's pool, skiing today's run and so on. Imagine yourself accomplishing whatever specific task is in front of you. Run through that difficult turn, recite that powerful line, whatever challenge awaits. Play this imaginary performance in your mind as many times as it takes to get comfortable. By the time you're actually competing, you should know exactly where your tough spots are going to arise and exactly how you're going to handle them. Your mind offers you the opportunity to run the course as many times as you need to before leaving the gate. It is your key to an Olympic stadium, to Carnegie Hall. It is your unlimited practice time. Use it and *be prepared*.

A NOTE ON ANXIETY

Like imperfection, anxiety is *a part* of competition and performance, an organic aspect of the process. What you experience as anxiety in performance is essentially a high dose of adrenaline being released at a time when you cannot fully make use of it. The result is that some of this hormonal energy is left coursing through your veins without a defined purpose. Accept it. As long as you are in the game, anxiety is going to be in it with you. Get to know it. Ask yourself, where is it in your body? Is it in your chest? Your solar plexus? Your legs? What does this thing I have been so afraid of actually feel like? Anxiety is not a good or bad thing, simply a part of this thing called performance.

Would you waste your time trying to get rid of your nose, accusing it of being in your face's way? Anxiety is as much a part of performance as your nose is part of your face. It is not something that must be crushed in order for you to do your best. It is your body's "ready" light, its way of telling you that it's ready to go, that what it is about to do matters to you. Just like your nose, your anxiety is supposed to be there. Stop trying to get rid of it and start living with it.

STAYING PRESENT

Earlier I spoke of the feeling that occurs in "the zone," specifically, that of disappearing into an altered sense of time and place, of not being there in the "normal" sense. There is another kind of disappearing that occurs in performance, and it is one that is neither productive nor enjoyable. In contrast to "the zone," when "not being there" is actually a state of acute awareness and presentness, there is also a state of "not being there" that is tantamount to sheer blankness or nothingness, as if you had been anesthetized before walking onto the stage. It is not just your judging, interruptive mind that leaves the scene in this scenario, but *all* of you. I have heard this state described as "death," "the void," "paralysis," "coma" and "sleep."

Are you often left wondering where you "were" during the performance, where your mind and you "went" during those important moments? Do you question why you weren't able to apply that which you've practiced? Do you get angry at yourself for "leaving the scene" at the moment when your presence was most needed? Do you often feel as if your mind and body empty out all of its contents (all of you) before walking onto the stage, leaving you with nothing but an anesthetized shell with which to perform? This is "not being there" in its most dangerous form.

The capacity to stay present *within* the performance, to not "check out" on the experience that is happening in that moment, this is a skill of top competitors. Staying present not only gives you the opportunity to enjoy the experience, but the wherewithal to make decisions as your performance is taking place (a necessary component of success). If you identify with this kind of "not being there" at times, if you walk off the stage in a daze, not knowing where you've "been" for the last hour, the following exercise may help.

THE FEEL

Choose a specific physical sensation associated with your craft. Periodically, throughout your performance, focus your attention solely on that sensation. Using something you can physically *feel* is usually the most powerful for this exercise, but you can experiment with sound, smell and anything else that your body experiences. At various points in your performance, actively turn your attention to this *specific* sensation, something you have decided on *before* the performance. For example, you might want to concentrate on the feel of the saddle against your thigh, your blade on the ice, the diving board under your toes, the soles of your feet against the floor, your hands on the piano and so on. The only important thing is that it be specific, something your body is experiencing in that situation. This will immediately bring your mind into the present moment (where the sensation is happening), and thus, return your focus to what you are doing. Remember, your body is always in the present. Unlike your mind, your body cannot exist anywhere but in the present. When you place your attention on something your body is experiencing, you bait your mind back into right now and precisely what you are doing on that stage. You cannot be "spaced out" when you are truly "in" your body. Use your body as your access to the present, your key to staying "there," your magnet for keeping your attention in your game.

CHECKING IN

Every so often during your performance, check in with yourself by asking "Am I here right now? Is my attention focused on my task? Where am I at this moment?" No matter what you discover, the simple act of asking will pull you back into the moment and encourage your attention to return from wherever it is. The important thing is to get in the habit of doing the asking. Make "Where am I?" and "Am I paying attention to what I'm doing?" a part of the game plan for each and every performance.

BREATHING

Most of you have probably heard about the importance of breathing for relaxation. You may not however, understand how breathing relates to relaxation (other than if you don't do it, you are certain to be anxious.) You may have been told to *watch* your breath as a means of calming yourself. Unfortunately, the practice of simply watching your breath can leave too much room for your mind to think about and thus intensify your anxiety. The process of simply letting your thoughts pass may prove to be too difficult in the moments of pre-performance anxiety. A more active role for your mind is often preferable. When anxious, it is helpful to have a specific place to *put* your mind, something active to *do* with it, to *concentrate* on, a destination to house your frantic attention.

As with all exercises, you must practice *regularly* at home, and *not* simply on the day of competition. Once you are anxious is *not* the time to begin your breathing practice. The time to teach your body to relax is when you are calm. How can this be? If you are already calm, how can you practice your reaction to stress? Doing your breathing exercises when you are relaxed provides your body with a physical memory of calmness. Your body learns to associate this state of calm with particular breathing exercises, to link the breathing with the state that accompanies it. Once you are stressed, at the point when your body would ordinarily not be susceptible to relaxation attempts, your breathing will instinctively trigger this link, returning your body to its "practiced" state of calm. As your anxiety increases, your breath has a tendency to rise up in your chest. You may feel that your breaths become progressively more shallow, as if you can't get the air down into your lungs. You may feel that your nose closes off, allowing air to come only through your mouth. Without knowing it, anxiety makes you take more frequent breaths (in response to this feeling that you can't get enough air). The result is a state of hyperventilation with the unpleasant symptoms of lightheadedness and tingling limbs. Hyperventilation may also leave you feeling slightly disconnected from your own body, as if you are spinning somewhere outside yourself. All of this creates even more anxiety and thus the cycle perpetuates itself.

Become an expert on your own breathing and the spiral of reactions that breathing sets off. First, pay attention to the specific way your breathing changes when you encounter stress. So too, notice how your body responds to those changes, and most importantly, what *your mind* does with those physical sensations. Get to know your own breathing and reaction cycle. Awareness marks the beginning of your taking control of anxiety.

Becoming conscious of your own breathing is a way of establishing an immediate connection with yourself. Paying attention to your own breath allows you to check in on your internal state, to go inside instead of running farther away, and thus to break the habit of abandoning yourself in moments of need. To turn your attention to your breathing is to say "Hello in there. I'm here with you and I'll stay with you through this." Use your breath (and your attention to it) as a means of joining and grounding yourself, particularly in those moments when you feel scattered and without a firm sense of self.

EXERCISES

In a moment, I will introduce several breathing exercises. If possible, do your breathing exercises everyday. A few minutes for each is enough, but the more time you can practice your breathing, the better. Notice how the different techniques affect you. Which calms you? Which slows your breathing? Centers you? Agitates you? Energizes you? Notice *your* body's reactions to these exercises. Once you know your reactions in practice and at home, begin to incorporate the appropriate exercises into the day of performance. As you get more comfortable with the process of manipulating your breath, you will be able to use the techniques right up to and even during performance time. Keep in mind, once you have "locked in" a particular technique, it will only require a few seconds of your attention to elicit a response from your body.

Find a quiet place (preferable but not necessary). Pull your focus *inward*. Bring your attention to your breathing. Simply become aware of it. Let your mind address your breathing as it would a thought or conversation. Initially, do not try and manipulate your breath, just notice what it's doing. Think of your breath as you would a swing. The only place where *you* have a task is at the top of that arc, at the moment when the swing momentarily pauses. This is where you come in, to give the swing a nudge by initiating an inhalation or exhalation. The rest of the process is done without you. On its own, the swing moves effortlessly through its arc. You stand on both ends but get out of the way for the ride. So too, you need not decide when to draw in or let out your breath. Let your body *ask* for the air it needs and inform you when it has enough. Your task is to get still enough to hear your body's voice.

For all exercises, the inhale is taken in through the nose, the exhale out through the mouth. Get in the habit of holding your in and exhalations for as long as you can. (It will allow you to feel the arc.)

1. DIAPHRAGMATIC BREATHING

Begin by placing one hand on your belly. Concentrate on breathing very slowly *into* your hand, focus on making that hand rise with your breath. This is not an exercise in pooching your stomach out. Rather, focus on filling and expanding your belly with air. Concentrate all of your attention on the area just below your navel. Bring your breath *into* this place, imagine your breath filling it up as if it were a balloon.

Once your hand is rising and falling without great effort, move the focus of your attention to your back. As if you were a bellow, imagine (and feel) the air opening up your lower and mid-back, expanding into your sides and spreading open your lower ribs. Feel your sides growing wide.

Use your breath to expand your entire mid-section: belly, lower-back, mid-back, sides and ribs. See and feel your entire center opening as you fill the area with your breath. Imagine a wide seat belt around your middle. Feel its weight and presence. Breathe *into* that belt; feel that belt expanding with each inhalation. Experience and welcome the calm that resides in this center of your body.

2. CIRCULAR BREATHING

Imagine that your lungs are made of three sections: a lower, middle and upper chamber. Visualize your inhalation beginning in the lower chamber of your lungs. Hold it there for a couple moments, feeling it in the bottom of your chest. Ever so slowly, pull the air up and into the middle chamber, pausing again. Finally, draw it up into the top of your lungs. Allow your shoulders to rise a bit as the air reaches the upper part of your chest. Hold it. At each stage, concentrate on seeing and feeling where your breath is residing within you. Now exhale through your mouth. As you do, visualize your breath as a stream of light (whatever color you chose). See it leaving your mouth. Hold the exhalation a couple seconds beyond the point when your body asks for more air. Do this exercise until you feel that you are simply allowing your breath to move through you, guiding it in an effortless circle.

3. SPINAL BREATHING

Sit or stand very straight. Imagine your spine very taut and strong. Picture your breath as a ball of luminescent light at the base of your spine. See it there. In your mind's eye, tie a golden thread onto that breath and very slowly, pull the ball up through your spine, Imagine this ball as a pool of sparkling crystals, weightless, cooling each vertebrae as it passes through it. Focus on feeling this sparkling light rising up your back. Continue pulling the breath upwards with your golden thread, up the back of your neck and skull until it reaches the very top of your head. Hold this breath and light at the top of your head for a few moments (as long as is comfortable).

As you exhale out through your mouth, imagine that you are pushing that same breath down the front of you, into your neck and throat, down through your chest, and eventually all the way into your lower belly. As the light sinks down into you, imagine it getting heavier and bigger. By the time it lands in your belly, it should feel as if you are holding a baby made of breath. Hold this exhalation and fullness for as long as you can, feeling the strength of that breath in your center. You now have the task of moving that bundle of breath back into the base of your spine for its next launch up your spine. As you get ready to initiate your next inhale, see this bundle sinking down and backward at a slight angle, deep into the base of your back. Visualize this shift, as if the air were sliding backwards into your tail bone. The breath is light and weightless once again as you begin your next inhalation.

4. ALTERNATIVE BREATHING

Using one hand, place your thumb on one of your nostrils. Take your index and second fingers and place them on your forehead (optional.) Close the nostril your thumb is covering. Breathe deeply through your open nostril. Cover your open nostril with your ring finger. With both nostrils closed, hold the inhalation for a count of seven (or as long as you can). Keep your ring finger closed and now open your thumb (releasing the first nostril). Exhale through this open thumb-nostril. Hold the exhalation for the count of seven. Repeat the exercise, inhaling through this thumb-nostril while keeping your ring finger covering the other side. Close both nostrils as you hold the inhalation. Now close your thumb and open your ring finger. Exhale through this open side. Continue the cycle for at least 10 long breaths.

5. THE EASIEST BREATHING EXERCISE OF ALL

There is no exercise as easy and with such a giant payoff as the simple deep breath. Don't take it for granted! When you are too anxious to think about anything, much less moving your breath this way or that, force yourself to at least take a few deep breaths. This is something you can do anywhere, anytime, which requires very little concentration. For as easy as it is, the deep breath produces dramatic results.

You already know how to do it, but keep the following in mind:

a. Inhale though your nose with your mouth shut.

b. Hold the inhalation for at least a few seconds.

c. Exhale through your mouth, lengthening and exaggerating the release of air.

d. *Sigh* as you exhale.

e. Imagine squeezing out every ounce of air from your lungs, as if you were wringing out a sponge. Exhale until you have squeezed out every drop of air left in you.

f. Hold the exhalation for a couple seconds beyond when your body asks for more air.

6. THE LAST HOPE

When no breathing technique seems possible, when your anxiety reaches a fever pitch and internal bedlam arrives, there is still one card you may be able to play, your joker, so to speak. *Sing.* I don't care who's around you, just sing whatever comes to mind (even if it's just words about how nervous you are). If you can get to your car, crank the radio and start belting it out. While you're singing, try to *move* as much as you can. When you're anxious, your instinct is to stop moving. The body mimics the mind by freezing which then intensifies your anxiety. Think of what your body does when it gets cold, how it wants to hunker down and assume hibernation mode, to conserve its energy by standing still. The truth is, only by moving will your body get warm. Such is the case with anxiety. *Do* something to release it. Singing (preferably loudly) does just this; it releases the excess energy and oxygen. In those moments when nothing else can, singing gives your breath, and thus your anxiety, a place to go.

REAL GOALS

Write down your list of goals—do not simply say them out loud. By putting them on paper, you make them *real*. Be specific, goals are not vague. What *exactly* do you want to achieve? By when do you want to have achieved it? Where do you want to be, how do you want to feel, what do you want to be working on, and what do you want to have done in one month's time? How about three months? One year? Amend your goals as you change and grow. Always take note of reaching a goal. Never take an accomplishment for granted. Do something different when you reach a goal, even the smallest one. Give yourself the praise and reward you deserve. Do something kind for yourself. Stay on top of your goals. Be aware of where you are in relation to them, set up time markers (every X number of months) at which point you will mark your progress, determine how close or far you are from achieving your goals and what, if anything, you need to change.

One trick: As you walk out onto the court/stage, try telling (and convincing) yourself that you are the performer who has already achieved your goals (whether this is true or not). Trick yourself into believing that you are the tennis player who won last year's Wimbledon, the actor who won last year's Academy Award. Sometimes a little mind game, one that tells you that you have already "done" it, can help you actually "do" it.

I WANT IT

Practice saying "*I want it.*" Say it, yell it, sing it, be it! Allow yourself to feel your own desire as you say the words. Repeat them over and over and before every performance. Give yourself permission to get "pumped" about what you want. The simple repetition of the words "I want it" enhances your motivation as well as your competitive edge. Get comfortable with your own desire. Don't swallow it, enjoy it. You are allowed to want it. You've got to want it. Your ambition is a powerful tool. Welcome it. Celebrate it. Your body can hear you. It hears you when you say you *can* do it and it hears you when you say you *want* it. Announcing and reminding yourself how much you *want it* will help you get it.

I CAN DO IT

Remember the little engine that could? Put your cynicism on the back of that engine and watch it ride away. It may be hard for you to believe, but something as simple as *telling* yourself that you can do it (no matter how strongly you believe your own words) *will help* you do it. I *can* do this, I *can* do this, I *can* do this." Keep at it. Whether you know it or not, you are listening.

HOW WAS I BETTER TODAY?

After each performance, make a list of things (mental or physical) that you did better on this day. What aspects of your game were improved? How were you different and better? No matter how disastrous the overall performance was, if you have to sit there for an hour to think of one thing you did better today, sit there for an hour and write it down. Keep these improvements together in one book and make it a part of your training, not only to do the writing, but also to periodically re-read your "Better Book" (and take note of your own progress and the long road you've traveled).

CHANGE

Change creates change. When in doubt, *change something*. It's not so important what you change, just that you change something. Alter your program for no other reason than to shake up the *old* system. Your change may not seem like the perfect solution, it may not even seem remotely appropriate or connected. You need not know exactly why you're doing it, but a new approach offers possibility solely on account of it being new.

A diver who was having problems with his entry on a key dive illustrates the point. In a last ditch effort to keep his coach from taking the dive out of his program (and after toying with every aspect of the dive itself), he decided to change the way he walked out onto the board (before getting into position). "The two have nothing whatsoever to do with each other, but I'll give you your change," he muttered sarcastically to me on the day he decided to give change for its own sake a try. He never did figure out how the two were related, but with the new walk, he entered the water flawlessly (and without a splash) on practically every attempt. Needless to say, he got to keep the dive in his program. Give up on trying to control the "outcome," on always trying to understand the what and why of it. Change is not about specifics, it is about the larger shake-up of the old system. Regardless of whether you fully understand its purpose, change offers the potential for growth; it offers hope. One change alters everything that follows it. It forces you to do things in a new way, and this is what you want. Change, no matter what it involves, is a catalyst.

FIND A ROLE MODEL

Choose a performer you admire, someone whose skill and style excites you. It's not important that this artist be the best, just that she's someone who performs the way you want to, that something about her particular style appeals to you. Make it part of your training to watch her perform. Seize *every* opportunity to observe her. Watch how she walks onto the stage, how she begins her game, handles adversity, victory, mistakes, everything about the way she moves and plays. Let yourself soak in her way, drink in the overall picture. Try not to describe her to yourself as you watch her, not to break her down into isolated movements and words. Simply allow yourself to watch. Observe her often enough so that your body can, without thinking, evoke the perfect image of her. Flash on her image before and even during your game. You should be so familiar with her way of moving that it begins to feel like a part of you. Is there is a specific move of hers that you particularly love, something that grabs your attention, that "juices" you? If so, *copy it*, make it *your* move too.

Pride has no place here—don't waste your time with it. You are not stealing but merely modeling yourself after your image of excellence. Observing and mimicking those performers who are further along than you should be a part of your regular training. There is nothing so powerful for your body as to *see* what you want it to do. Use all the resources available to you, particularly the example and expertise of those who do it better.

CLUTCHING

Here's the good news: the act of clutching is usually preceded by thoughts of clutching. "I know I'm going to blow it," "I never come through in the clutch," "I'm no good under pressure," "I'm not the one that should play now," "I can't be trusted," "Let someone else do it," etc. As hideous as they are to listen to, such thoughts are in fact a good thing; they are your warning signals. Your error is in believing that these thoughts must become reality, that they are, inevitably, a self-fulfilling prophesy. This is *not* the case. Your self-sabotaging thoughts need not lead to self-sabotaging behavior.

Expect your clutching thoughts. When you know a pressure situation is approaching, know that such thoughts are going to emerge. Once you are there in your performance know that the internal dialogue may continue. Just as an ex-smoker knows that he will crave a cigarette when he takes a drink, so too, you know that these clutching thoughts are your reaction to the perception that it "counts." The ex-smoker expects the craving, takes note of it, but chooses not to indulge it. Expecting such thoughts helps to deactivate their power. Without the element of surprise, their arrival is nothing more than a bit irritating, not to mention boring and sad (given that you have to listen to them).

Give your clutching thoughts a name. When they appear, say to yourself "Oh there's Jane doing that Jane thing." Once you have identified the voice, ask her to leave (or if need be) tell her to leave. Once you give her a name, she may pass more easily. Should she not want to be so cooperative, imagine something happening to Jane, see her jaw sewn shut or her head burning in flames. Find an image that helps you silence her voice. Use your clutching thoughts as a signal to re-focus your attention on the present and your task at hand. Turn your attention to what you have been working on in practice. At the same time, conjure up an image of the successful you or an experience when you felt confident. But as with everything, be prepared.

VISUAL REALITY

Video can help. Whenever possible, tape your performances. Video forces you to witness what *actually* happened when you were out there. The process of watching yourself will help you to become aware of your propensity to exaggerate your own failings. Chances are, what happened is *not* what you imagined. When you can watch (or hear) your mistake as it looked or sounded in reality, see it for the simple over-arched back, fumbled chord, eye-off-the-ball event that it was, you will see your mind's power to distort and exaggerate, to create something enormous and grotesque out of that which is small and benign. So too, by watching/

hearing yourself on video/audio, you are forced to be in contact with all the things you did right.

Regardless of how you attempt to invisibilize and discount these positive elements (and you will), at the very least you will have let them physically scan across your eyes. You may find it amazing that these things you did right still managed to show up on tape considering the presence of your mistake. You will expect to see/hear only your error, magnified a thousand times in slow motion, over and over, with nothing else from the performance on either side of it. As you watch yourself, notice the actual amount of time the mistake occupied in relation to the entire performance. Become aware of the *reality* of what the mistake looked like. The mistake that appears on tape (unlike the one in your mind) has a beginning, middle and *end*. It lives and dies in that instant on the stage. It does not, as you imagine, wear you like a robe of shame long after you have left the scene of "the crime."

Video will show you the mistake the world saw. You will be forced to see the performer you are as opposed to the image of yourself you have in your mind. This is not to say that your mind won't try and invalidate what your eyes see. It will. But the process of seeing/hearing yourself as you actually appear can provide a reality check for your mind's distortion. In this way, your eyes and ears can assist your mind in developing a new image of who you are. You may find yourself surprised by how much you do know, how much you have learned despite your refusal to give yourself credit for the work.

Furthermore, if you are inclined to berate yourself for your mistakes while still performing and/or are unable to recover within your performance once you have "fallen" from perfection, video can serve yet another purpose. In the words of a client, "The reality of my image on film showed me how small and specific the *original* mistake could have been. It allowed me to see the parameters and time frame of the mistake itself, the event which later became the glue for my attention and set off that all too familiar performance-destroying spiral. I can see where it *could* have ended and how I chose to offer it the long life it enjoyed. The video allowed me to distinguish between *it* and the giant, all-consuming event that *it* became in my mind and hands. Watching the reality showed me how much time and space there *could* have been to erase it, to recover, had I been able to leave the original mistake where it actually happened. Essentially, how much good time *could* have followed my one bad moment. It really didn't have to turn into a disaster; it actually could have been a great concert!"

THE EMOTIONAL HOOK

Your memories, whether of people, music, events, places or anything else you've experienced, generate certain feelings in you. Perhaps there's a song that "gets you psyched," a person who made you really believe in yourself, a coach's saying that pumped you up, a particular place that made you feel alive, an accomplishment that made you feel especially proud. Choose one of these experiences to use as your motivational hook. You are going to call up this image whenever you feel your drive fading, fatigued, unmotivated, or any other "dead" state. It is not important what the image is, just that it be a personal memory, one that when you think about it, returns you to your positive feeling state at that time.

Now in the same way that you did with your motivational hook, search your memory for the experiences (or people) in your life who made you feel intensely confident, strong, calm or any other state of mind you want to be able to generate in performance. The idea is to create a "bank" of memories and images from which you can draw in order to fire-up whatever change of state is needed.

Keep in mind, it is important to have chosen your images before competition. Have them ready to go. Take advantage of the remarkable connection that exists between your mind and body, and more specifically, the incredible power your memory has to change your internal state.

YOUR GOLDEN BALL

In those moments when you feel afraid, small or tired, imagine a golden ball of fire or light within you. In these states of smallness, call on your flame for strength and energy. Create an image of your golden ball. See it shimmering, filled with light, heat and energy. Take your attention into it. This energy is you. It is always there, burning and sparkling, always available to you. See your ball. Feel its presence; believe in it.

A LAST NOTE ON TECHNIQUE

Your attention is the most powerful tool you possess. Being able to decide where you put your focus is what creates greatness. When you start *choosing* where to direct your attention, you are harnessing the greatest source of power within you.

Keep in mind, the techniques I've outlined here are just suggestions, practices that have helped either my clients or myself. There is nothing set in stone, however. If watching your negative thoughts fly away on the wings of birds' works for you, then the wings of birds it shall be. If you find that your breathing exercises are helpful the morning of competition but distracting just before you walk on the court, by all means, do them in the morning. There are no rules, just that you try. The idea is to discover what works for you, to become an expert in your own mental training. Sensorizations are very personal. Your version of a golden box of sun might be a river filled with jewels. I encourage you to invent your own golden box, filled with the sensorizations that work for and inspire *you*. Spend the time and energy to do this. It *will pay off*

EPILOGUE

Most folks spend their whole lives not only in quiet desperation but in mediocrity, unwilling and unable to really go after something, to go the distance inside and out. Why? Because it's that hard! Don't kid yourself, greatness demands the courage to do things that are extraordinarily difficult, sometimes terrifying. It insists that you be willing to be humbled, infinitely, by your craft, to come face to face with every demon that lives inside you, to confront your past and present and all the players in it, to fall down again and again and never stop getting up, to admit, endlessly, that you do not have the answer, to commit, endlessly, to finding that answer, to put yourself and your pride permanently on the line, to accept that something is bigger than you, and to be able to just keep at it!

Each time you are forced to stretch, to leave your comfortable perch, to reach inside yourself and find more (even when it feels like there isn't any more there), to dig deep and rise to another challenge—remember—this is precisely your test. Your passion is asking you if you have what it takes. Do you possess the courage that greatness demands? Are you brave enough to stay with it no matter what or how much is asked of you? Those who choose this path must have the heart to walk it. One thing is for sure: it takes great courage to live with great courage. Have it, be it, live it!

RECOMMENDED READING

1. Gendlin, Eugene T. *Focusing*. New York: Bantam Books, 1982.

2. Cornell, Ann Weiser. *The Power of Focusing: A Practical Guide to Emotional Self-Healing*. New York: Fine Communications, 1999.

3. Kabat-Zinn, Jon. *Wherever You Go, There You Are: Mindfulness Meditation in Everyday Life*. New York: Hyperion, 1995.

4. Jackson, Phil. *Sacred Hoops: Spiritual Lessons of a Hard- wood Warrior*. New York: Hyperion, 1996.

5. Rotella, Robert J. *Golf Is Not a Game of Perfect*. New York: Simon & Schuster, 1995.

* For more information on some of the techniques discussed in Chapter 7, "Overcoming Negativity," contact The Focusing Institute at www.focusing.org.

If you would like to order another book or reach the author, please contact:

Luminous Press
2565 Broadway, #185
New York, NY 10025
Phone: 212-316-6648
E-mail: LuminousPress@ultinet.net